C1184

Ideology
and the Rise
of Labor Theory
in America

Recent Titles in
CONTRIBUTIONS IN LABOR HISTORY

Ideology and the Rise of Labor Theory in America

___ John A. DeBrizzi _____

Contributions in Labor History, Number 14

GREENWOOD PRESS
Westport, Connecticut • London, England

Library of Congress Cataloging in Publication Data

DeBrizzi, John A.
  Ideology and the rise of labor theory in America.

  (Contributions in labor history, ISSN 0146-3608 ;
no. 14)
  Bibliography: p.
  Includes index.
  1. Industrial sociology—United States—History.
2. Labor economics—United States—History. I. Title.
II. Series.
HD6957.U6D4 1983   306'.36'0973   82-12024
ISBN 0-313-23614-3 (lib. bdg.)

Library of Congress Catalog Card Number: 82-12024
ISBN: 0-313-23614-3
ISSN: 0146-3608

First published in 1983

Greenwood Press
A division of Congressional Information Service, Inc.
88 Post Road West, Westport, Connecticut 06881

Printed in the United States of America

10 9 8 7 6 5 4 3 2 1

Copyright Acknowledgment

The author and publisher are grateful for permission to
reprint from John R. Commons, *Myself* (Madison, Wis.: The
University of Wisconsin Press, 1936).

For the Wing

Contents

Tables

___ Acknowledgments _____

THE EARLIEST IDEAS AND RESEARCH for this book were joined when I attended the State University of New York at Buffalo. In Buffalo, Professor Morris Fried, a truly outstanding teacher, impressed upon me the significance of the labor movement for both the development of modern society and the discipline of sociology. This project is as much his as mine. Although there are some views herein with which Professor Fried may disagree, I hope that there is much more that will receive his approval.

Many colleagues provided me with invaluable assistance and encouragement. Sincere encouragement for this project, especially at a time when the situation about me grew ominous, was forthcoming from Professor Veljko Rus at Research Committee 10 of the International Sociological Association. Dr. James Sabin of Greenwood Press provided assistance in bringing about the completion of the book. His guidance and cooperation made things uncomplicated.

Diane Williamson supplied a great contribution by translating my writing into the form of a manuscript and saving my sanity on a number of occasions. The cooperation of Kathy Monteverdi, despite incessant demands on my part, permitted me to meet deadlines and finish things in a most pleasant frame of mind. The wing, as always, was inspiring.

Ideology
and the Rise
of Labor Theory
in America

1 Introduction_____

SOCIOLOGICAL ANALYSES OF THE WORK of the early American sociologists have been few and far between.[1] Though most sociologists have some familiarity with the efforts of their intellectual pioneers, this seldom extends beyond an acknowledgment of the general reformist inclinations present within early American sociology. Precisely what the early sociologists were attempting to reform, or what directions their efforts took, is rarely considered in depth, if at all.[2]

The tendency to consider the reform impulse of early sociology in general terms is exhibited in the work of C. Wright Mills:

> In the last half of the nineteenth century, social science in the United States was directly linked with reform movements and betterment activities. What is known as "the social science movement—organized in 1865 as the American Social Science Association"—was a late nineteenth-century attempt to apply science to social problems.[3]

In a recent work, the Schwendingers were somewhat more specific in their comments on the early sociological reformers:

> Corporate liberals [among whom the authors include early sociologists] argued that without political regulation of economic life, capitalism would be destroyed by class conflicts involving militant labor unions and socialist movements on the one hand, and gigantic monopolies

or monopoly trusts on the other. They also argued that laissez-faire liberal doctrines had to be revised substantially because they opposed the expansion of the capitalist state.[4]

It was the case that the early sociologists in America were concerned with the rise of socialism and militant unionism. During the decade of the 1880s, a number of American universities became the homes for scholars, including those identifying themselves as sociologists, interested in the labor movement of the day.[5] It was in the 1880s that a distinct body of literature on trade unionism in America came into existence. Among the most influential of these early works were Richard Ely's *The Labor Movement in America* and George McNeill's *The Labor Movement: Problems of Today* (1886 and 1887, respectively). Franklin Giddings, later to hold the first chair in sociology to be established at Columbia University, contributed a chapter to the latter volume.[6]

Giddings's concern with labor was not idiosyncratic. Other early sociologists were also very much interested in the problems associated with an expanding capitalist industrial system: the demise of rural society and the rise of urbanism, the growth of organized labor and the large corporation, and immigration.[7] As Charles Page indicated: "The pioneer sociologists, living through those tumultuous years, naturally entered a large share of their attention on the problems of class conflict."[8]

In view of the above, the interests of early American sociologists cannot be considered as unique or exceptional when compared to the interests of European sociologists of the late nineteenth century.[9] This is readily apparent if one notes that sociology in America emerged from a reform movement within the discipline of political economy. According to Page, the early American sociologists represented "the left-wing of the new economists."[10]

The new political economy as a movement arose in reaction to the dominance of the laissez-faire perspective within economics. It sought to establish itself as an accepted part of university studies and advocated a thorough investigation of contemporary social problems. The foremost of those problems was the growing labor movement and the attendant class conflict in America. It was during the 1880s that the new political economy first found a home at Johns Hopkins University, then under the presidency of Daniel Gilman.[11] There, during the latter part of the decade, theoretical concern with the labor movement was firmly established through the efforts of Richard Ely, who with other proponents of the new political economy came together to organize the American Economics Association in 1885.[12]

However, not until the 1890s were departments of sociology organized within the universities and even then, there were but a few.[13] Sociologists did not form their own professional organization until 1905, a full twenty years after the political economists had done so. Given these facts it is not surprising that at the time sociology was established as a discipline within the university the "founding fathers" were nonspecialists in the field. Most of them, in fact, were trained in economics.[14] Albion Small and E. A. Ross, two of the most renowned of the early sociologists, were trained under Ely at Johns Hopkins.[15] In effect, prior to the twentieth century there was simply no hard and fast line separating political economy and sociology. As late as 1893 Richard Ely helped to form the American Institute for Christian Sociology.[16]

It was not unusual, therefore, before 1905, for a scholar to be accurately referred to as a political economist or a sociologist, and to have shared a common concern and interest under each title. This is why an appreciation of the new political economy and the early labor theorists is necessary for an understanding of early sociology in the United States. This is especially true with regard to the primary interest of those scholars—the labor movement in America. The intent of the early labor theorists was to reform American capitalism to enable it to cope with the threat they perceived in the labor movement.

Among the most renowned of these new political economists was John R. Commons. With regard to labor theory he is surely the most widely known today. No doubt this is largely due to the fact that Commons's work, especially as popularized by his founding of the so-called Wisconsin

School, has become the most accepted and influential theory of the development of the labor movement in the United States.[17] It was the Commons-Wisconsin theory of labor in America that presented the thesis that American society was unique or exceptional when compared to European societies. The many implications of this thesis will be analyzed in detail in this study.

The fact is that early American sociologists did not, themselves, have unique or exceptional interests when compared to their colleagues in Europe, and Commons's notion of American uniqueness is based upon a weak foundation. Assumptions about the special character of American society have never been supported fully by well-documented research.[18] Despite this, unfortunately, contemporary sociologists have expressed no interest in studying the development of early labor theory or the reasons for the influence of Commons's ideas. The lack of attention is especially distressing in that the development of early labor theory represents an extremely interesting and integral aspect of the development of sociology in the United States.[19]

This study will analyze the development of labor theory by considering it as a social activity subject to the influence of the class interests, culture, and the social conflicts that existed in the general society. Through this perspective, one may realize that the acceptability of a theory may be determined on grounds other than the internal structure of the theory or the weight of evidence used to support it. In brief, a sociological theory may gain acceptance not simply because it provides the most adequate explanation for a phenomenon but, rather, because the explanation it does offer arrives in a form that is particularly appealing.

It is the thesis of this work that the Commons version of labor theory gained recognition not so much for what it explained about the labor movement (other theories did better on this score) but, rather, for how it explained the movement. That is, the Commons theory was couched in a form that proved to be particularly appealing. The social analysis supplied by John Commons incorporated into the realm of

theory a good deal of the "common sense" of its day.[20] Like
common sense, the theory never was fully coherent. It stood
fragmented and contradictory. Yet, it was the very lack of
coherence that provided the appeal of the theory; particular
social groups found it an easy task to make of Commons's
ideas much what they chose to in order to secure their own
interests. In this regard, a good measure of the recognition
granted to Commons was due to the affinity his theory shared
with the interests of different social groups.[21]

Unfortunately, what Commons intended for his theory and
what his supporters made of it were not in conformity. Indeed,
Commons's project, intentions, and ideas eventually were lost
in the myriad of interpretations that were forthcoming from
those who employed the product of the theorist to satisfy
their own needs to their own greatest advantage. Virtually
all of early labor theory in America was promulgated by
scholars drawn from the ranks of the traditional middle class.
The early theorists shared a world view, basic values, and the
same project. However, it was the Commons version of labor
theory that most distinctly and clearly expressed the traditional middle-class ideology.[22] What that ideology encompassed
has been largely forgotten; along with it have been forgotten
the dreams and hopes of a middle class futilely attempting
to understand and survive the era of industrial capitalism in
America.

The early sociological theories of labor in America are sus-
ceptible to misinterpretation when the social and ideological
contexts from which they emerged are neglected. The intentions of the early theorists and, indeed, the meaning of their
projects, are confounded when they are not viewed as part
of a traditional middle-class effort to come to terms with the
changes introduced to society by a process of capitalist industrialization. Thus, contemporary scholars continue to engage in a rather abstract and pointless debate over whether
Commons and the other early theorists were liberals or conservatives.[23] They were both. They were liberals to the extent that they desired to reform some of the social processes
operative in American society. They were conservatives in

that they wished to perserve the contours of a capitalist system and the parameters of wealth and power therein. As Commons would put it, they wanted to "preserve capitalism by making it good." In order to comprehend their notion of "good," however, it is necessary to understand their backgrounds and values, and the social situation that their theories addressed. An effort to provide that understanding is the focus of this work. The reasons the Commons version of labor theory came to enjoy paramount recognition may then be more easily understood.

In the following pages it will be shown that the emergence of labor theory was related to the exacerbation of class conflict in America. This will be provided through a historical analysis of the development of political economy in the nineteenth century. Analysis reveals that the American social structure did give rise to class conflicts and that early sociologists were intensely interested in that phenomenon, especially with regard to its manifestation in the labor movement.

The labor theories of Richard Ely, Henry Carter Adams, and John Commons will receive careful consideration since these theorists shared the same project. All of them operated from a world view that emerged from backgrounds in the traditional middle class, and each of them propounded their theory from a similar set of values. Ely, Adams, and Commons were contemporaries and familiar with each other, and there was a degree of intellectual exchange among them. Ely served as a teacher to the others and each came to the personal assistance of their colleagues on a variety of important occasions.[24] In fact, Commons's theory of labor relied heavily upon the earlier ideas of Ely and Adams.

In that the world views of Ely, Adams, and Commons were essentially the same, and since Commons's theory of labor depended upon the work of the others, it can be demonstrated that the primary advantage enjoyed by the Commons version of labor theory was the affinity it shared with the interests of particular social groups. It is particularly significant that business interests perceived an affinity with Commons's theory.

The questionable basis of Commons's thesis of American exceptionalism is revealed by the fact that the political sympathies of organized workers in the United States were associated with the social conditions of industry rather than an inherent uniqueness of American society. The manner in which Commons's theory of labor assumed an affinity with the interests of business and other social groups will be documented. The reasons that the theories of Ely and Adams did not gain recognition will be explicated.

Finally, the significance of the academic basis of Commons's theory, its eventual institutionalization as the Wisconsin School, and later developments within the Wisconsin School will be discussed, along with a consideration of the utility of this study for contemporary American sociology.

2 The Old Economics: Political Economy __ Prior to 1885 _____

IF ONE CONSIDERS THAT LAISSEZ-FAIRE economic theory indicates the belief that the operation of market forces assures, by virtue of natural, immutable law, the most efficient and beneficial socioeconomic order possible, there can be little doubt that laissez-faire and political economy are virtually synonymous before 1885.[1] This was the old economics. These two terms were so closely associated in the American mind that the latter may be considered as a somewhat systematized rationalization of the former. Richard Hofstadter succinctly described this relationship:

> The accepted function of political economy, as taught in American colleges and propagated in the forums of opinion, was apologetic. It had always been an idealized interpretation of economic processes, under the competitive regime of property and individual enterprise.[2]

For one interested in more specific indications of the relationship between political economy and laissez-faire, it is fruitful to consider the relative popularity of the various schools of thought in economics. Popularity serves as a gauge of the impact that an idea has had on a population—a useful consideration since the diffusion of ideas may then be judged as either relatively wide or narrow.

If this consideration is confined to the academic world, it becomes clear that the principles of laissez-faire did provide the most prominent perspective in courses concerned with the substance of political economy. Jean-Baptiste Say's

Treatise on Political Economy, which was basically a sys-
tematized presentation of laissez-faire doctrine, was the most
popular economics textbook in American colleges up to the
Civil War era.[3] At a later date, popular texts were written by
American proponents of laissez-faire. Arthur Latham Perry's
Elements of Political Economy and Amassa Walker's *The
Science of Wealth* were highly regarded representatives of
this type.[4] The most popular economic tracts among the general population from 1865 to 1880 were the works of Adam
Smith, John Stuart Mill, and Arthur Perry.[5] Thus, concrete
evidence attests to the primacy of laissez-faire within American political economic thought in both its academic and popular forms. Why was this the case?

In essence, it appears that the assumptions of social benef-
icence and natural harmony inherent in laissez-faire were not
immediately challenged by American experience. No salient
denials of the laissez-faire claims could be grounded in the
everyday operation of the United States as a political-economic system. This is not to deny that there was evidence of
disharmony in the American economy prior to 1880. Indeed,
the history of the American worker indicates that strikes,
protests, and economic reverses were not rare even in the
early nineteenth century.[6] Yet, such evidence could easily be
interpreted as deviant cases which only served to accentuate
the dominant characteristics of the economy up to that
time.[7] This view is clarified when one realizes that at the out-
break of the Civil War the United States, by today's standards,
was still basically an "underdeveloped" nation, that is, the
American economy was primarily agricultural. Investments in
manufacturing constituted just one-seventh of those in agriculture.[8] Furthermore, the major manufacture in the America of 1860 was the processing of farm products; the foremost
industry of the day was the refinement of flour and meal.[9]
In this sense, then, the assumptions of laissez-faire remained
unproblematic because they were not truly put to the test in
the context of a modern economy.

If one factor was viewed as giving rise to disharmony in the
operation of the free market system it was the incompleteness or underdevelopment of the system itself. William Tudor,

an English observer of the American business scene during the first quarter of the nineteenth century, surmised that

> The cotton manufactories are numerous; they are scattered over every part of these states . . . these are, in almost every instance, the property of incorporated companies. . . . The aggregate of their produce is very considerable, though very few of them continue in full steady operation. Their capital is commonly too limited to enable them to transact their business advantageously. They are often obliged to make forced sales of their goods, and a rise in the price of the raw material consumes all their profits, and forces them to suspend their work; of course, they cannot be expected to make any great improvement, while liable to such operations.[10]

In effect, then, the problem hampering the beneficent operation of the economy was the restricted nature of the market system due to the restricted supply of capital. Accordingly, the hallmark of modern production, the factory system, remained undeveloped. Thus, though production within the factory did exist, it was not representative of the state of manufacture in the antebellum United States.[11] This situation contained two contradictory implications for the proponents of laissez-faire.

On one level, in the United States, as a self-sufficient nation state, the laissez-faire doctrine appeared to capture the essence of the situation in its belief of natural harmony. That is, in terms of social integration, the nation experienced no immediate contradiction between the concepts of employer and employee. As Norman Ware observed, the denial of the idea of this community of interest was first to be found among factory operatives.[12] To the extent that factory organization was not greatly developed, neither was the idea that the free developments of the economy might introduce elements of conflict and disharmony into the nation. Viewed in this light, the doctrine of laissez-faire constituted more of a promise for the future than an explanation of the then contemporary economic system in the United States.

This idea may be understood if one recognizes that the laissez-faire doctrine was imported directly from Britain. What was modified, however, were the implications of the doctrine. English political economy culminated in the pessimism of David Ricardo's "iron law of wages." However, American economists' version was that such a "law" was inapplicable to the American situation. That is, American adherents to laissez-faire believed that the free operation and development of the economy would not necessarily result in the material degradation of the worker.[13] For example, remuneration for unskilled labor in England and America before the Civil War differed in that such wages in the latter state were from 33 to 50 percent higher than in the former.[14] What permitted this discrepancy in wages to exist was the availability of relatively cheap land. In terms of a utility theory of wages, then, workers would not find attractive any wage which was, at a minimum, any less than the rewards which flowed from one's efforts in independent agriculture. What the American laissez-faire proponents forgot was that the higher wage rates in their nation could prevail only as long as the availability of land remained unchecked.

The basis for higher wage rates tended to collapse as the opportunity to engage in independent agriculture diminished. Thus, the promise of laissez-faire in America was destined to be broken. What is important, however, is that prior to the post-Civil War era it had not yet been denied and, therefore, at least appeared to be tenable. One may say, then, that the advocates of laissez-faire were optimistic that the free development of the economy, when coupled with the special conditions found in America (which they assumed to be constant rather than variable) would bring the best to all in the nation, employer and employee alike. The harmony that prevailed at one point in time was projected into the future as a normal course of development.

When the various class groups within the United States were considered, the free operation of the economy did not seem to impair their harmonious interaction with one another. This, however, was primarily a reflection of the essentially undeveloped nature of modern production and not the consequence of laissez-faire per se. Aside from this matter, the underdeveloped economic condition of the nation possessed implications not at all favorable to the laissez-faire perspective.

When one came to consider the reason for the underdeveloped nature of American manufactures it became clear that the lack of capital was a primary factor.[15] This was a condition relating to political economy, not on the national level, but on the level of a world system. Accumulation of capital in America was impeded by the subordinate position of United States manufactures vis-à-vis their British counterparts. This situation was itself a product of laissez-faire and, as such, at least logically, seemed above criticism.

It is clear that as long as this condition did exist, the promise of American laissez-faire could never be fulfilled. The progress of industry was stymied by the competitive advantage enjoyed by the English. According to the logic of laissez-faire, the United States was destined to be an agricultural supplier to an industrialized Britain. Yet, according to its promise, laissez-faire was to afford the harmonious and full development of America's economic potentialities. These two points constituted a distinct contradiction which most political economists of the time did not clearly perceive. It was not surprising, therefore, that for the most part political economists in America were solidly aligned with the classical doctrines, including a commitment to the idea of free trade—the very proposition which, if faithfully followed, would prolong the United States' occupation of a subordinate position within the world market system.[16]

This contradiction was perceived, however, by at least one American political economist, Henry Carey. In this sense, he represented a source of originality within the economic thinking of pre-Civil War America.[17] Carey contended that free trade was a policy concocted by England with the intention of promoting its industry at the expense of other nations where manufacture was in a comparatively immature stage of development.[18] His suggested remedy was the institution of a protective tariff which would provide a shelter for young industries.[19] Paradoxically, Carey, despite his advocacy of the

removal of a cornerstone of laissez-faire doctrine, maintained
a belief in the essential validity of laissez-faire policy, including "true" free trade. As he put it in 1852,

> It has been asserted . . . that protection tends to build up
> a body of capitalists at the expense of the consumer, and
> thus produce inequality of condition. That such is the
> effect of inadequate protection is not to be doubted. So
> long as we continue under a necessity for seeking in
> England a market for our surplus products, her markets
> will fix the price for the world. . . . Inadequate and un-
> certain protection benefits the farmer and planter little,
> while the uncertainty attending it tends to make the rich
> richer and the poor poorer, thus producing social and
> political inequality. . . . All, therefore, who desire to see
> improvement in the political condition of the people of
> the world should advocate the system which tends to
> break down monopoly and establish perfect freedom of
> trade.[20]

Thus, although Carey recognized the contradictory implications of laissez-faire for America on an immediate, practical
plane, he was never able to grasp the problem theoretically.
He did not seem to recognize that the inconsistencies with
which he was forced to grapple were representative of the inconsistencies of the developing economy itself. The problem
was not caused by something external to the economic system, but was part and parcel of that system. That is, the contradictory implications of laissez-faire in America were a
microcosmic representation of the disharmony produced by
a world economy premised upon laissez-faire capitalism. Marx
summed up this matter in a most succinct fashion when he
commented on the evolution of political economy after
Ricardo:

> . . . with Carey—the harmony of the bourgeois relations
> of production ends with the most complete disharmony
> of these relations on the grandest terrain where they ap-

pear, the world market, and in their grandest development, as the relations of producing nations. All the
relations which appear harmonious to him within specific
national boundaries . . . appear as disharmonious to him
when they appear in their most developed form—in their
world market form. . . .

Where the economic relations confront him in their
truth, i.e. in their universal reality, his principled optimism turns into a denunciatory pessimism. This contradiction forms the originality of his writings and gives
them their significance.[21]

It appears that as long as the American economic system
remained comparatively undeveloped, any disharmony or conflict might be projected toward an outside or foreign influence
in that it was not conceived to be a flaw inherent to laissez-
faire but, rather, attributable to nationalist politics.[22] Only
with the advancement of industrial development would it become clear that laissez-faire capitalism was, itself, a source of
problems and disharmony within the American political-
economic system. Only then would a substantial working
class emerge upon the national landscape. The conditions of
the time, however, did not yet clearly reveal these problems
for all to see. It ought to be noted, in addition, that until the
end of the Civil War the great majority of Americans were
self-employed.[23]

The preceding comments are not to be taken to indicate
that the United States was devoid of industrial enterprise
prior to the 1860s but rather, that this was not representative
of the economy as a whole. Save in the textile and iron manufactures, industry was small scale in the sense that it did not
operate with much machinery, employed few workers, and
could be initiated with a small amount of capital—an amount
small enough to be commanded by a single entrepreneur.[24]
The Civil War stimulated the growth and expansion of extant
industry. One may gauge the intensity of this stimulation by
considering the average yearly incorporations as presented in
Table 1. (Only the states for which complete data are available
are included.)

TABLE 1
Yearly Average of Incorporations in New Jersey and Massachusetts
per Decade, 1850-1899

	New Jersey	Massachusetts
1850-59	14	19[a]
1860-69	12	76
1870-79	46	78
1880-89	386	154
1890-99	1,135	233

[a]Average is based upon total number of incorporations, 1851-59.

Source: George Evans, *Business Incorporations in the United States,*
    1800-1943 (New York, 1948).

It is of note that New Jersey and Massachusetts were among
the few states that enacted general incorporation statutes before the Civil War. This is significant since such legislation
served to indicate that manufacturing concerns had assumed
a size and technical sophistication which demanded a level of
capital investment usually beyond the capacities of a single
proprietor or a few partners.[25] As may be seen in Table 1,
the yearly average of incorporations in the decade immediately prior to the Civil War was less than twenty. However,
by 1870 to 1879, the yearly average was already almost three
and one-half times greater than the prewar figure in New Jersey, and over four times greater in Massachusetts. By the
1880s the yearly average was almost thirty times as great in
New Jersey. In Massachusetts the rate was eight times that
of the prewar decade.

The rather large difference in the rates of increase between
the two states is partially explained by the fact that New Jersey had a liberal general incorporation statute. That is, it was
very favorable to the large corporation in terms of the state's
taxation policy and expeditious incorporation procedures.
Thus, since incorporated firms were assuming a greater size
in terms of authorized capital stock (reflecting a greater ex-
penditure on machinery and plant), it was to their advantage

to seek a New Jersey charter. One may observe this phenomenon in Table 2.

It may be discerned in Table 2 that while there tended to be a significant difference in capitalization levels between the two states in the war decade, that difference became even greater in the postwar decades. In the most favorable political climate of New Jersey, each succeeding decade witnessed a significant rise in the average capitalization of incorporated firms.[26] As one may readily calculate, the average capitalization was almost double that of the war decade by the 1880s.

While the factory organization of manufacturing clearly existed prior to the Civil War, it was not developed but rather basic and immature save for a few industries. However, after the war, judging from the increasing popularity of the corporate form of business organization, which became necessary in terms of the new levels of investment demanded, the political-economic system itself may be said to have experienced a qualitative change. Indeed, by the 1880s the average capitalization of the 386 yearly incorporations in New Jersey approached the half-million level (see Tables 1 and 2).

The implication of this situation, as indicated earlier, was that modern business, dependent on extensive capital outlays for machine and plant, now involved a group of investors and was usually beyond the capacity of a lone entrepreneur. Where business success at an earlier time was associated with individual initiative, it now depended primarily upon organi-

TABLE 2
Average Capital Stock Authorization in Massachusetts and New Jersey per Corporation by Decade, 1860-1899

	New Jersey	Massachusetts
1860-69	$250,000	$168,000
1870-79	310,000	97,000
1880-89	491,000	66,000
1890-99	666,000	43,000

Source: George Evans, *Business Incorporations in the United States, 1800-1943* (New York, 1948).

zation. In the postwar decades the problems of organization did not arise from the corporate form itself. The corporation as a business form existed before the war and, later, simply expanded both vertically (in terms of the average investment per corporation) and horizontally (in terms of the increased frequency of corporate charters issued). The real organizational problem in the decades following the war concerned the combination of corporations or, in other words, the trust.[27] This corporate combination united not only formerly separate producers but also introduced the large investor or promoter as an important figure in the advanced circles of the business world. The trust was, in one sense, the original structure that provided for a community of interest between producers and financiers. Though it began in the 1880s, this combination of financial (investor) and industrial (producer) capitals reached its most potent partnership at the turn of the century.[28]

3 The New Economics: Political Economy __ after 1885 _____

IN THE LATE 1870s THE UNITED STATES experienced what was
later characterized as the most bloody and violent labor history of any industrial nation in the world.[1] The so-called
Great Awakening of 1877 brought the indigenous conflict
between capital and labor to the attention of the nation. Beginning on the Baltimore and Ohio Railroad in West Virginia,
strikes and riots spread across the land to the Pacific coast.
In Pittsburgh and St. Louis, workers almost seized control of
the entire cities. The great armories which now stand in America's large industrial cities are a monument to the fear that the
outbreaks of 1877 aroused among the upper classes.[2] Norman
Ware described these effects as "enormous":

> For the first time in America the head of labor revolu-
> tion was raised. . . . Labor became an outlaw, the wage-
> earner a member of a subcommunity or class, separate
> and distinct from the general community to which he
> had, at least in theory, always belonged. Credence was
> given in fact to the "un-American" theory of class war.[3]

For the first time, then, the movement of labor in America
became a national concern. What was earlier assumed to be
nonproblematic—the relations between employer and employee—became, by force of circumstance, something of overwhelming and significant import. Further discredit to the
laissez-faire promise of harmonious development arose from
the severe depression beginning in 1873 which was nearing
its end when the 1877 outbreaks occurred. The two events

were, of course, related. In the final years of the economic
stagnation, 1877-1878, three million workers were unem-
ployed and, as a result of business failures, at least 20 percent of the working class faced permanent idleness.[4] Indeed,
the depression was the primary source for discrediting laissez-
faire theory because it gave rise to two conditions—a disgruntled and angered working class and the beginnings of the
"trustification" of industry—events which denied the validity
of the harmony of interests and free competition.

The situation is understood when it is realized that the
catalyst for the Great Awakening consisted of wage cuts
prompted by the attempts of industrialists within the railroad
industry to reduce costs during a period of continually falling
prices. In fact, prices continued to plummet for almost twenty years. As V. S. Clark acknowledged, "It was the desire to
stem the steady reduction in prices, among other things, that
encouraged the formation of industrial trusts."[5] Accordingly,
the long depression contained forces inimical to laissez-faire
on two fronts.

Given the situation above, it was not surprising that laissez-
faire began to be questioned as an adequate perspective for
political economy. Though most economists still could be
classified as proponents of laissez-faire, certain revisions were
clearly discernible in some quarters. Especially significant in
this regard were the ideas of the economist Francis Walker
(1848-1897), son of the noted proponent of laissez-faire,
Amassa Walker. He was among the first to recognize that political economy needed to concern itself more with the new
facts which exploded onto the social scene and less with the
rationalization of current beliefs and practices.[6]

As is usual with thinkers in a period of transition, his
ideas were somewhat ambiguous; they looked backward at
one moment, only to appear progressive at another. For
example, Walker tended to split the newly formed community of industrial and finance capital into "good" and "bad"
factions, while failing to recognize that it was such a community of interests that colored the character of the new age.
The captains of industry, or entrepreneurs, were "good" in
his eyes because they actually produced profit and value while

the "capitalists" or financiers were "bad" in that they produced nothing, but simply sought gain in speculative investment. On the other hand, Walker appeared to realize that a new day had dawned, since imperfect competition was now characteristic of the marketplace. Due to this, he suggested that State interference in the interests of labor was permissible, though only to restore the ideal of perfect competition.[7]

Though he still considered himself a laissez-faire economist, Walker was representative of the rise of revisionism and the departure from orthodoxy. The significance of Walker's ideas is that they illustrated the manner in which the drastic changes occurring in the economic structure of society could prompt a rethinking of the formerly sacrosanct statements of political economy.

One should be cautious here and realize that the beginnings of revisionism were not simply an immediate reflection of changes that occurred in the economic substructure of society. Rather, the economic changes that have been considered to this point should be thought of as a subterranean river flow, surreptitiously eroding the foundations of laissez-faire political economy. Alterations in theory did not occur at random, as one would expect in the case of immediate reflection of substructural changes, for example, as in an earthquake in which entire structures crumble to the ground haphazardly. Instead, revision in political economic theory was of a conscious, rational sort. That is, the changes in political economy were partly a result of political economists reflecting back upon earlier ideas and comprehending their inadequacies in terms of new social conditions.

The greater significance of revisionism is best understood by realizing that prior to the Civil War there was no distinct course of study in the area of political economy in the United States. Instead, the content was presented in the context of courses on "moral philosophy."[8] Thus, political economy came close to assuming the status of morality; laissez-faire was perceived as true in an absolute and timeless sense. Self-reflection was absent, with self-assurance as its surrogate. Reflection on the state of theory only arose when the discipline constituted itself as a science rather than a moral system. This development had to await the rise of postsecondary education in America and this came only after the Civil War. Until that happened later substantial revisions in political economy were to come from scholars, such as Richard Ely and Henry Carter Adams, who were exposed to new and competing ideas during their studies in European universities.

It is not surprising that change occurred in the postwar era. Significantly, it was fostered by a process of self-reflection, which indicated that political economy was becoming more of a science and less part of a system of morality. An affront to morality often serves simply to strengthen a particular system of morals. Revision of premises, however, is a product of critical consciousness and this latter attitude is more aligned with a scientific turn of mind.

The growth of universities after the war and the emergence of new disciplines, such as political economy, were essentially a result of the tremendous upsurge of industry and the import of science to it. That is, as society progressed in terms of the industrialization process, new needs arose which had to be served by the expanding system of higher education, primarily by graduate education.[9] Now, the changes which had been considered earlier called for a new turn of mind appropriate to the new age. While the structural changes in society indirectly sanctioned the new modes of thought, the revisions in political economy were the result of the new ways of thinking, not the direct and immediate results of economic changes alone.

Direct and outright opposition to the laissez-faire approach to political economy came from the so-called new economics. This perspective in political economy decried the abstract and rationalizing formulations of laissez-faire and demanded that the discipline become involved with contemporary problems of the economy and the issues that arose from it. Whereas the old economics might be characterized as primarily abstract and moralizing, the new approach emphasized the concrete study of pressing social problems. What was especially irksome to those advocating the new approach was the extreme individualism inherent in laissez-faire and its consequent inability to consider the explosive labor problems of the day in anything other than an offhanded manner.[10] Though political economy was changing, the change was not fast enough for the new economists.

It is notable that the proponents of this new approach to political economy all grew to maturity in the long depression that followed the economic collapse of 1873.[11] In one sense, they were between two worlds. Though reared in the world of traditional nineteenth-century middle-class America, they were confronted by a world which was coming to deny the values and beliefs with which they were inculcated. To their inquiring minds, laissez-faire appeared totally inadequate in terms of providing an understanding of the changing society, especially with regard to the enormous growth of the labor movement. It is also significant that the new mode of thought brought to political economy by the new economists was not originally nurtured in the United States but in Europe. Thus, while American conditions opened the door to revision in political economy, the intellectual foundations for a definitive critique were to be found abroad. How important that influence from abroad was is obvious: two of the three major interpreters of the labor movement in America were trained in political economy in Europe. After being graduated from Johns Hopkins in 1878, and having attended the lectures of Francis Walker there, Henry Carter Adams traveled to Europe to complete his professional studies.[12] Likewise, Richard T. Ely undertook his study of political economy in Germany at Heidelberg, where the renowned Karl Knies was his major professor.[13] Of the three chief early interpreters of the labor movement in America, only John Commons was educated solely in this country. This, however, was only possible due to the foundations built by his professional predecessors.

Commons studied under Ely at Johns Hopkins when the latter returned from Europe. It was while at Johns Hopkins that Ely helped to popularize the new approach to political economy, an approach heavily influenced by his study within the German historical school of economics.[14] The historical approach was also important in the development of the ideas of Henry Carter Adams and John Commons.

Only when the new way of thinking was constituted as part of political economy in the American university system did the new economics present an effective and viable alternative to laissez-faire. In fact, the American Economics Association (AEA), an organization originally founded to advocate the approach of this new economics, was not established until 1885. It was at that time that the historical-institutional approach to political economy became a part of graduate education in the United States.[15]

Derived as it was from the German historical school, the proponents of the new economics in America argued against the existence of immutable natural laws in the economic and social worlds. To them, society was an evolving organism whose variable and shifting nature would not permit the existence of laws independent of particular points in history. That is, any laws that existed were shattered as the objective conditions which gave rise to such regularities were modified in the course of historical evolution. In short, they took economic and social laws and theories to be relative rather than absolute.[16]

The new economists criticized laissez-faire as an ideological doctrine, not consciously designed but, emerging as a result of historical evolution. That is, the new political economists viewed particular propositions of laissez-faire, such as free competition as a natural regulator, as possibly accurate at one point in time, but having been rendered inaccurate as a result of social change. Thus, what might have been a valid generalization premised upon the social conditions which existed in the past was now, once those conditions were modified, a misrepresentation of reality. This notion was brought to explicit expression in Henry Adams's presidential address before the AEA:

> The mistake of English political economy . . . does not lie in the emphasis it gives to competition as a regulator of commercial conduct, but in its assumption that the bourgeois conception of property was ordained by nature and on that account, lay outside the influence of evolutionary forces.[17]

Following from this belief in the relativity of economic law was the correlative belief that the primary constant in the social world was man himself. That is, the true subject for study was not the abstract and timeless laws of laissez-faire, but man in his changing social world. Where laissez-faire was content to maintain a focus upon supposedly timeless laws, the new economists argued that man and his changing needs should be the primary object of study. This meant that contemporary social problems, if economically relevant or conditioned, were a legitimate area of study.

For the new economists, laissez-faire could not consider the new social problems because of its a priori and deductive nature. Furthermore, because of this nature, laissez-faire could not offer any concrete and practical solutions relative to such problems. Contrary to such an approach, the new economists argued for rigorous analysis based upon an empiricism supplemented and broadened by a historical perspective. In their minds, this served to indicate that an analyst had to remain cognizant of the social context of the matter being analyzed. This approach was later to be termed the "institutional approach."

In short, then, the major complaints against laissez-faire were its a priori, static, and individualistic biases. It is worthy of note that such criticisms were not confined to political economy but, in fact, appeared to be the common critique proposed in many new intellectual currents in the United States of the last quarter of the nineteenth century. The ideas of Lester Ward and Charles Peirce's reconsiderations in philosophy indicated that there was a general intellectual upheaval coincident with the new social conditions arising within the nation.[18] It appeared that the old social fabric was becoming tattered—the old ways of thinking and acting no longer appeared appropriate under new social circumstances. In a sense, the basis of social order was itself threatened by the incompatibility of the old and the new. The entire society may be viewed as increasingly tending toward anomie.

One goal of the new economists was to restore stability and consistency to the social order. To them, the practicality of the new approach lay in its assumed ability to constitute a rational basis for the formation and direction of industrial society. This was something that laissez-faire, by its very nature, was perceived as unable to do.[19]

What made the labor movement appear as the primary problem American society had to face was the growth of the organized movement after the 1873 depression and the escalation of labor-related violence thereafter. Also of concern were the revolutionary elements which came to be considered as part of the developing American movement. Various revolutionary societies of immigrant workmen had sprouted since the 1850s following the arrival of refugees from the European revolutions of 1848. Though these elements did not represent any sizable portion of American workers, their ideas were considered potentially dangerous. When strikes and violence did occur the blame was often (though generally inaccurately) laid upon the heads of foreign agitators. In some instances, however, the connection between the labor movement and foreign leadership did exist and such cases, especially when there was violence, made a strong impression on observers and analysts.[20] All of this emerged into the public spotlight within a relatively short period of time.

The wave of strikes and riots that appeared in 1877 was noted earlier. In 1879 the Socialist Labor Party was formed with the intent of politically organizing the American working masses. In 1882, a notorious anarchist, Johann Most, arrived in the United States and began to preach the extermination of all capitalists and oppressors. Most was a frequent visitor to Chicago and attracted a significant following among working people there. Albert Parsons, a prominent Socialist Labor Party leader, took up Most's views and attempted to popularize them among a wider audience. [21]

In addition, the most important national organization of American workers of the time, the Knights of Labor, experienced a phenomenal growth in an extremely short period. In 1879 the Knights had 9,287 members; by 1880, already 28,136 had joined; in 1883 membership increased to over 51,000; and by 1886 they had enrolled nearly three-quarters of a million workers.[22]

The year the Knights moved toward the million-member

mark also witnessed the Haymarket bombing incident, which served to cement the link of labor organization, strikes, and violence in the public mind. One concrete sign of growing unrest may be obtained from the Commissioner of Labor's figures, which reveal the tremendous growth of strikes during the 1880s.[23] These figures indicated the following:

Year	Number of Strikes
1881	471
1882	454
1883	478
1884	443
1885	645
1886	1,411

Though there was no necessary connection between all the aforementioned events, the timing of the events assured that such connections would be assumed by most observers. As a result, "the labor problem" came to represent the entire pattern and was of special concern to the new political economists. One of the primary thrusts of their new approach was the formulation of an interpretation of the growing labor movement in the United States.

It was during the same period that the American Federation of Labor (AFL) was organized. Though originally overshadowed in terms of membership by the Knights of Labor, the Federation represented a hard-headed militancy, unlike the inconsistent policies of the Knights. As William Dick demonstrated, the early AFL under Samuel Gompers followed a course which may be interpreted as reflecting an acceptance of Marxian principles. In sum, the early Federation conceived of itself as working for the abolition of capitalism.[24]

This attitude and policy was reflected in Gompers's statement to European labor leaders: "Comrades, though oceans divide us, the same spirit and purpose prompts us to seek in organization the final emancipation of the Proletariat of the World."[25] Thus, the first stable nationally federated organization of American workers appeared to represent something more than a demand for higher wages. It possessed a goal similar to the revolutionary intentions of the European labor movement. It was at this time that the first theory of the American labor movement arose.

The general socioeconomic framework ought to be noted: the theory concerning the development of the labor movement was coincident with the rise of finance capitalism in the 1880s. The accumulation of surplus capital in the hands of American financiers depended upon the intensive growth of American manufactures which generated such surpluses. Prior to the 1880s, expansion of heavy industry in the United States was dependent upon foreign investment.[26] This development depended upon the industrialists' acceptance of outside leadership for the business enterprise. As a result of the overexpansion that precipitated the 1873 depression which, in turn, ushered in almost a generation of falling prices and profitless competition, industrialists were often disposed to accept such leadership. The intent of such a policy change was to bring about a period of peace in lieu of cutthroat competition and, thus, afford a return to business prosperity. Such prosperity depended, above all else, upon economic stability. The acceptance of outside leadership became more frequent as the generation of original "captains of industry" retired from the business scene.[27]

Thus, the first interpretation of the American labor movement arose at a time when a national organization of workers represented a stable phenomenon, when that organization appeared to present a threat to the political—economic system of the nation, and when finance capitalism was first emerging onto the scene. An appreciation of all these factors is important for an understanding of the development of the new political economy and, at a later time, the Commons-Wisconsin School of labor theory. It was precisely these factors that constituted a challenge to the world view of traditional, nineteenth-century middle-class America.

4 Richard T. Ely
and the Search
__ for a New Morality _____

IT IS IN THE PERSON OF RICHARD ELY that one encounters the
first new political economist and the first academic to devote
serious attention to the problem of the growing labor movement. His book, *The Labor Movement in America*, which appeared in 1886, represented the first in a train of academic
treatises which took as their foci of interest a range of related
problems that emerged within the developing American political-economic system.[1]

Though the early work of Ely on labor was criticized as
containing "superficial research and much moralizing," it
clearly served to break new ground in its day.[2] In addition,
the early ideas of Ely continued to influence later theorists,
and Ely, himself, was personally responsible for launching the
academic career of the then relatively unknown John Commons at the University of Wisconsin.[3] Thus, in addition to
representing the first of the new economists and labor theorists, Richard Ely was a central figure in the development of
the Commons-Wisconsin School of labor theory. Were it not
for the efforts of Ely, the Wisconsin School, as it is known today, might never have existed.

Born in Fredonia, an upstate rural community of New York
in 1854, Ely was brought up with a strong emphasis on religion.
His original vocation, under the tutelage of his father, was for
the ministry.[4] Toward that end, Ely won a fellowship from
Columbia University to study philosophy in Germany in 1877.[5]
At the University of Halle, however, another American student,
Simon Patten, introduced Ely to Professor Johannes Conrad, a

leading figure in the German historical school.[6] From that
point on, Ely directed all his energies to the study of economics.
Upon returning to America in 1880, Ely took up a position
at Johns Hopkins University where he remained until 1892.
Thereafter, he assumed a position at the University of Wisconsin.[7] Richard Ely's experiences at Wisconsin were of great
importance. It was there, in 1894, that Ely was charged with
attempting to undermine the faith of students in American institutions, and in propagating socialism and anarchism.[8] Though
exonerated by the university's board of regents, Ely was severe-
ly disturbed by the episode. Thereafter he changed his views
and pronouncements on the labor movement and virtually
abandoned his studies of labor and trade unionism and focused
his interest toward developing a land economics. He maintained that interest up to the time of his death in 1943.[9]
Ely throughout his life maintained a deep admiration for
German scholarship and administration. As one commentator
expressed it, for Ely, "Germany served as an enviable bench-
mark from which American achievements in reform and research could be measured."[10] A Germanic influence was clear,
even at the time of the Wisconsin episode (1894), when Ely
opined in an article that he considered the State to be a "divine" institution.[11]
Although the early religious influences in his life may not
be discounted, this particular view held by Ely appeared also
to derive from his student experiences in Germany during the
late 1870s. One of his early students complained in a diary that
Ely's "narrow little mind had become so steeped in German
prejudice" that he found it difficult to find anything of use in
English political economy.[12] In essence, then, Ely appeared to
accept the basic premises of the German historical approach to
economics completely and without criticism.
It would seem that this total acceptance of the new economics (as the German historical approach later came to be known
in America) on the part of Ely was the result of the almost
complete absence of earlier experience with economics. Unlike
the other political economists who will be considered later, Ely
had very little exposure to advanced economic thought prior to

his travel to Europe. In fact, he originally set out upon his journey to Europe in order to continue his studies in philosophy.
Only after his disillusionment with philosophy, the urgings of
friends, and his meeting with Johannes Conrad at Halle, did he
enroll in a graduate program of study in economics. He did so
at Heidelberg in 1878 under Karl Knies, a major thinker within
the German historical tradition.[13] In short, Ely's commitment
to the Germanic viewpoint on economics was due, in part, to a
comparative lack of exposure to competing ideas at an earlier
date. Also, one may not dismiss his earlier interests in religion
and philosophy, which predisposed him toward a moralistic
consideration of social life.

There is ample evidence to attest to the connection that existed between Ely's moral views and the theological ideas of a
host of German thinkers. As Benjamin Rader acknowledged,
"Ely's primary appeal as teacher and economist lay in his strong
ethical commitments."[14] Ely expressed his ethical impulse as
follows: "There is within man an ethical feeling . . . clarified by
religion, telling us that in our economic life as well as elsewhere
we must seek to promote the welfare of our neighbor and
brother."[15]

This moralistic temperament was also apparent in Ely's participation in a group known as the American Institute of Christian Sociology.[16] As Ely related his involvement with this group
in his autobiography, the intent of the organization was clear:

> We regard the State as an educational and ethical agency
> whose positive aid is an indispensable condition of human
> progress . . . [the development of society] has brought to
> the front a vast number of social problems whose solution
> is impossible without the united efforts of Church, State,
> and Science.[17]

It is clear that Ely tended to view the then current problems
facing America through a moralistic lens. Furthermore, Ely's
ideas, as witnessed by his participation with the "Christian sociologists," were directed toward the goals of brotherhood,
welfare, and harmony. All these goals were attached to the
conception of the State as a "divine" institution and, thereby,

served to legitimate State activity in the affairs of civil society. This, in fact, was a basic premise of the German historical school of economics.

In one sense, then, the American movement that advocated the Social Gospel was an indigenous representative of this Germanic priniciple. One is not surprised, therefore, to discover that Ely maintained many connections with the Social Gospel movement. In fact, Ely's *The Social Aspects of Christianity*, published in 1889, became standard reading for Protestant social reformers near the end of the nineteenth century.[18] Thus, it is clear that Ely was not simply a reformer but, more to the point, a Christian reformer who believed that the State was a divine institution on earth whose task it was to harmonize the social order and set it upon a righteous path.

Ely's commitment to a general Christian principle as part of his social science represented a concrete link to, and a possible derivative of, his study of German economic and social thought. This was especially true of that aspect of German thought which represented the glorification of the State and bureaucracy. It should be noted that Ely's study in Germany coincided with the institution of the Bismarckian system—a connection that may be appreciated still further once it is realized that Ely's basic viewpoint fit squarely with what Hegel termed "the German Spirit":

> The destiny of the German peoples is, to be the bearers of the Christian principle . . . the History of the World, with all the changing scenes which its annals present, in this process of development and the realization of Spirit. . . . Only this insight can reconcile Spirit with the History of the World—vis., that what has happened, and is happening every day, is not only not "without God," but is essentially His Work.[19]

In effect, Ely substituted the American State for the "German peoples" and was to argue that the State must now act in accordance with its true nature. Thus, to one who considered the State as divine, and who foresaw its role as one of guiding society toward a proper course, it seemed only natural to be

"so steeped in German prejudices." What this meant in the specific context of America was that the State could no longer sit
idly by as it was expected to do according to laissez-faire principles of political economy. Instead, it was to encourage the
development of brotherhood and harmony among all social
groups. This was particularly the case with reference to the explosive quarrels involving capital and labor in an industrializing
society. In short, the State was to assist in setting the moral environment for the new era America faced.

What must be realized is that this new morality, for Ely,
could not arise through simple fiat but had to be discerned
within the bosom of the nation. That is, the State could not
invent the morality but had to encourage the development of
that morality which it assumed inherent in civil society. For
Ely, the greatest impetus to the Christian principle of brotherhood and harmony was the labor movement in the mid-1880s.[20]

The Knights of Labor were the most prominent representative of the movement of labor at the time of Ely's concern. For
Ely and the moral viewpoint, then, the Knights of Labor became the labor movement and the labor movement was the embodiment of the Christian principle. As such, the task of the
new economics was to explicate and encourage the growth of
the labor movement.

This represented Ely's point of view when he returned to
America from Europe and accepted a position at Johns Hopkins University in 1881.[21] Ely was to remain at Johns Hopkins
until 1892, and it was there that he began the first academic
inquiry into the labor movement of the United States. Since
the social conditions Ely confronted upon his return to America
represented the raw material for Ely's theoretical endeavors,
an understanding of that social setting is essential.

As a general characterization of the situation one may say
that American society was becoming dominated by large-scale
business interests. As C. Wright Mills described the era,

> The supremacy of corporate economic power, in a for-
> mal way, began with the Congressional elections of 1866,
> and was consolidated by the Supreme Court decision of

1886 which declared that the Fourteenth Amendment
protected the corporation. That period witnessed the
transfer of initiative from government to corporation.[22]

What might be recognized in a more specific vein is that the
1880s witnessed significant technical developments which kept
a pace with the development of the industrial system. The number of patents issued annually increased from an average of
13,000 during the decade of the 1870s to an average of 21,000
during the 1880s. More importantly, the total horsepower employed in manufacturing concerns was increased by 85 percent
in the 1880s. The ramifications of this meant that big business
was growing and more and more workers were losing their
craftsmanlike status to become mere machine-tenders.[23] In addition, one must not overlook the importance of those conditions enumerated earlier; that is, the great depression of 1873
had ushered in a generation of falling prices and assorted attempts to curtail them, especially in the form of the initiation
of trusts.[24] As one economic historian was to relate these developments at a later date:

> To those engaged in the struggle for business survival
> these phenomena were the result of competition. One
> way to be fit to survive was to cut costs by effecting
> economies through a larger scale of operations in manu-
> facture, transport and marketing.[25]

This overall trend had drastic implications for the social order. As Philip Foner indicated, "In the 1880's the foundation
was also being laid for the domination of finance capital in the
twentieth century."[26] The financier in industry first emerged
among the railroads, and as previously noted, economic problems within the railroad industry provided the catalyst for the
working class "awakening" of 1877. It was in the railroad industry that the normal channels of investment were first destroyed and the normal course of business thrust into chaos. In
the 1880s new investment sources and industry reorganization
occurred under the watchful eye of J. P. Morgan.[27]

The great strikes of the 1880s centered around the railroads and these industrial disputes provided the impetus for the phenomenal growth of the Knights of Labor. Most of the strikes prior to 1886 were of a defensive nature; that is, they were begun in resistance to the wage cuts which seemed to be the only recourse available to business in a depression-ridden economy. Between 1883 and 1886 the number of such strikes more than tripled. In that latter year, almost 1,500 strikes were conducted by hard-pressed workers.[28]

This was the general social situation Ely faced during the years immediately following his return to the United States. It was this situation which brought forth the Knights of Labor as the largest and most visible of labor organizations. In fact, in 1886 the Knights might easily have been mistaken for the whole of the labor movement because its membership (well over the half-million mark) and apparent strength greatly overshadowed all other extant labor groups. This situation was largely the result of the depression, for example, of the thirty national unions that existed in 1873, only nine remained by 1877.[29] Though this number increased to eighteen by 1880, it does not appear that these organizations accounted for more than 138,000 members.[30] The manner in which Ely interpreted these developments may now be considered.

As indicated earlier, Ely maintained that the emergent industrial system had to be set upon a path leading toward the Christian principles of brotherhood and care for the commonweal. One does not have to search far to comprehend the reason behind Ely's contention. The 1870s ushered in an era of severe depression which culminated in a decade of "trustification" and the introduction of a large assortment of labor-saving devices. The common denominator of these measures was the attempt to cut costs and install economies wherever possible—but the center of such efforts was to be found in the production process itself. The general pattern following the introduction of improved, labor-saving machinery appeared to be the replacement of skilled workers or journeymen with employment of women and children. Following the general diffusion of such technology throughout a particular industry, the reduction of wages to that for unskilled labor was carried through regardless of sex. In *The Labor Movement in America* Ely summarized this entire process with the phrase, "thousands of laborers became tramps, their daughters prostitutes, and their sons criminals. Reduction after reduction of wages followed."[31]

For Ely the current situation was perceived to be the very antithesis of morality. This was true not only in the narrow, literal sense of "forcing the daughters of workmen into prostitution," but also in the wider sense that it revealed society to be on a course of disintegration. That is, one social group prospered at the expense of another and appeared to care little for the disparity. Under the impact of industrialization, a whole society was divided into dissimilar parts with the consequence that the integrity of the whole was placed in jeopardy. Morality, for Ely, was very much connected to the idea of a holistic society.

This connection may be best grasped in the following manner. A society was moral to the extent that it was holistic, and in order to be holistic each social member had to view another as entitled to essentially the same rights and privileges as he himself was. In short, each member of society must be regarded as similar in terms of their rights and duties. This morality was unproblematic to the degree that social members were alike. In such a case, to deny rights to another was to deny rights to one's self. However, to the extent that social members were different they might come to be viewed as primarily a means toward another's end, and only that. The implication was that such persons were in a subordinate position and, therefore, bereft of equal rights. To Ely, the course of historical development demonstrated that the latter situation was the contemporary case. What is more, the situation could be traced to the unfettered workings of laissez-faire capitalism. As Ely put the matter, "Industrialism destroyed family and village ties which had earlier furnished the social basis for brotherhood, but it provided the opportunity to extend the range of ethical obligation."[32]

In what strikes one as a Durkheimian line of reasoning, Ely indicated that this new opportunity for brotherhood or morality could be found in the interdependent nature of industrial society. That is, "Men form more truly than ever before a social and industrial organism, whose numberless parts are in infinite variety of manner interdependent."[33] Thus, to the extent that all men were recognized as necessarily related to others, the interests of each depended upon the interests of the others. In this sense, then, a degree of similarity might be reintroduced among the diverse social members. The discernment of this similarity was the premise upon which a widened conception of brotherhood and morality might be founded. And all this was true in that cooperation of social members through their interdependence, which recognized at least a general similarity of interest, would replace unbridled competition which assumed that success called for the almost complete degradation of the competitor. The wage reductions so prominent in the era symbolized this condition of inequality and degradation; laissez-faire capital was the subject, while the wage-worker served as the object of the process.

Though laissez-faire political economy promised a harmony of interests, this was unfulfilled by the course of history. To the extent that its operation resulted in the amassing of the opposing groups of labor and capital, and gave rise to conflict, it was immoral. In that laissez-faire could only observe the present events and not act, it condoned the immoral state of affairs. It was the new approach to economics that was able to discern a basis of cooperation and, therefore, reveal its essentially moral nature.

As Ely understood them, labor organizations were not to be denounced but, rather, viewed as a necessary attempt by workers to regain their rights in society. To repress them was to continue with the errors of the past. A moral condition might only be restored when labor was viewed as a complement to capital. Toward this end, Ely often made it a point to encourage men of wealth and social standing to make a sincere effort at understanding labor and to apply "Christian" principles to the "labor problems." Instead of attempting to crush labor, they should seek to become part and parcel of the very movement that sought to reconstitute the order of things; in this manner their own influence and knowledge could be employed to the greatest advantage of society.[34] Since the labor movement sought to attain equal right, it represented an embodiment of what ought to be. As such, the labor movement furnished the major impetus to a new brotherhood of men.

It is extremely interesting to note the place of leadership to which Ely wished to assign wealthy individuals and businessmen in bringing about the new morality. In effect, they were asked to become leaders of the very movement which they were, until now, battling with all their energies. This, however, was totally consistent with the intentions of morality, and in the interests of the wealthy themselves, for, as Ely indicated,

> One of the saddest things about the history of oppression of labor . . . was the fact that when employers were dictating ever-harder terms to their men they were themselves crowded to the wall and compelled to fight for existence by the merciless competition among themselves. Oppression thus necessitated oppression.[35]

It would appear, then, that Ely was disposed toward the institution of what amounted to a cooperative society; indeed, this was the case. In many ways, he believed that such a state was inevitable. For example, he held that the corporation bore a resemblance to a limited monarchical form of government. By placing this view in the context of an evolutionary scheme, Ely was able to theorize that as limited monarchy fell between the political stages of despotism and democracy, so, too, the corporation had arisen between industrial despotism and the coming cooperativist or industrial democratic era.[36] In Ely's estimation, historical evolution assured the eventual institution of a new morality.

When the preceding points are taken into account, it is not difficult to determine why the Knights of Labor represented to Ely the rising sun of a new society, nor why he would identify the labor movement solely with the Knights. To the extent that society was immoral (and the explosive labor-capital conflicts of the mid-1880s served Ely as a barometer of this social disintegration) the policies of the Knights appeared to embody the essence of the new morality that he was describing and advocating. In short, the Knights of Labor seemed to Ely the objectification of the moral notion. Norman Ware, a historian of the labor movement, characterized the Knights in this way:

> It was to fight consolidated capital that the Order tried to create an integrated labor society to replace the isolated craft alliances and conventions of reformers that had preceded. . . . The Order tried to teach the American wage-earner that he was a wage-earner first and a bricklayer, carpenter, miner, shoemaker, after. . . . This meant that the Order was teaching something that was not so in the hope that sometime it would be.[37]

The Noble and Holy Order of the Knights of Labor was founded in 1869 under the leadership of Uriah Stephens. Originally, though open to all who received wages for a living, the Order was steeped in secrecy and intrigue to such an extent that it lacked any public program.[38] As John Commons noted at a later date, the primary intention of the Order was "to create a healthy public opinion on the subject of labor (the only creator of value), and the justice of receiving a full, just share of the values of capital it has created." Yet another thrust appeared to be "to harmonize the interests of labor and capital" and to "lighten the exhaustiveness of toil." All these goals merged well with the fact that the Knights foresaw no quarrel with "legitimate enterprise" nor any conflict with honest capital. Instead, they contended that certain men "blinded by self-interests" had violated the rights of others and "even violated the rights of those they deem helpless."[39] To later analysts, even this inchoate program was too idealistic.[40] Yet, for Ely the platform would appear completely natural and appropriate.

As indicated earlier, the Knights grew in numeric strength following the Great Awakening of 1877. As a result of the greatly increased interest in the organization, it was decided to lift the veil of secrecy that surrounded the group. Only a short time later (in 1878) the Knights for the first time came forth

with a public declaration of principles. That declaration pointed
to the "alarming development and aggressiveness of great capitalists" which, if permitted to continue, would "lead to the
pauperization and hopeless degradation of the toiling masses."
Foner has noted that:

> the platform advocated a bureau of labor statistics; co-
> operative institutions, both productive and distributive;
> reservation of public lands for actual settlers; weekly pay
> for employees . . . and among other things arbitration of
> labor disputes.[41]

Most importantly, the Knights maintained that the conditions they deplored could not truly be alleviated until a cooperative society had taken the place of the wage system. Due to
this view, strikes were viewed as rather senseless acts. In addition, the Order expanded the category of those eligible for
membership: after 1878, any person who either worked, or at
any time had worked, for wages might join. In effect, this
meant that the Knights welcomed employers as union members. In fact, under this broadened policy, the only exclusions
were that "no person who either sells, or makes his living by
the sale of intoxicating drink can be admitted, and no lawyer,
doctor, or banker can be admitted."[42]

Once one understands the program of the Knights, it is not
difficult to comprehend the reason for Ely's enthusiasm for the
organization. Ely and the Knights appeared to be in complete
agreement with regard to the following points:

1. The present industrial system was immoral in that it
   had brought about the degradation of the common
   man.

2. The only corrective was the establishment of a cooperative society.

3. As a means toward such an end, employers should be
   welcome into the workers' organizations as well as all
   types of toilers, regardless of race or sex.

4. Strikes are to be discouraged as they engender sense-
    less conflict.

5. Arbitration is a more suitable procedure for a morally
    based cooperative society.

The Knights stepped into prominence at a time when national trades unions all but disappeared under the impact of the
great depression. The Knights began their meteoric rise in the
1880s. For example, in 1879 the official membership of the
Order stood at slightly more than 9,000. By 1880 the membership increased by almost three times to over 28,000.[43] Thus,
to many surveyors of the industrial scene, the Knights of Labor
constituted the labor movement in the America of the 1880s.
While this was not strictly accurate (after all independent craft
unions of skilled tradesmen did exist) it is not difficult to understand why such an impression arose once it is realized that
the Federation of Organized Trades and Labor Unions, the
precursor of the American Federation of Labor, which attempted to organize workers strictly along trade lines, was all
but ignored by the workers at its inception in 1881. As William
Dick perceptively observed, "Most unions, like the miners, preferred to work within the existing Knights of Labor and regarded the Federation as a dual movement."[44]

The greatest working-class support for the Order came in
1885-1886 when it conducted a successful wave of strikes
against the Gould Railroad network. Because of intense worker
militancy, which the Knights helped to support, the railroads
were forced to roll back dictated wage cuts. This was no mean
feat for the Knights in that the Gould system was one of the
largest in the nation and accounted for about 100,000 miles of
railroad line.[45] However, the enthusiasm for the Knights
proved to be evanescent.

The policy of militant strikes, the very activity responsible
for the great upsurge in membership, represented a contradiction of the principles of 1878. In other words, the Order maintained that strikes were deleterious to the institution of a
cooperative society; arbitration was deemed to be a more appropriate tactic. This contradiction was recognized by the

leaders of the Order and soon corrected. For example, in 1886 the Knights took part in another strike against Southwest Railroad, part of the Gould network. The order to strike went out and was recalled twice, apparently due to poor negotiating tactics on the part of the Knights. In any case, after a citizen's group petitioned the executive board of the Order "in the public interest," the strike was officially called off. To most workers, this represented a needless and total capitulation by their leaders.

> The [Knights'] officers were so emphatically opposed to strikes that any sort of a settlement was preferable . . . in 1886 the control of strikes was placed in the hands of the executive board. . . . The intention, however, was not to manage strikes but to prevent them altogether if possible. . . . The settlement of the Southwest was an example of how far the general officers would go simply for peace.[46]

Thus, the policy of the Order appeared to stand in conflict with the developing desires of its membership. In part, this was due to the rather abstract nature of its principles—which were never quite translated into guidelines for everyday action—and to the extremely wide eligibility standards which permitted almost anyone to become a member. In addition, the heterogeneous nature of the membership meant that the abstract principles of the Order could be interpreted in a variety of ways, depending upon one's particular interest. The net effect could only be confusion. As Gerald Grob described the situation,

> The leaders of the Knights thus found themselves in a tacit alliance with rural elements. . . . The antistrike policy of the Order's leadership reflected a conviction that the condition of the working class could only be improved through the abolition of the wage system. Rural members, on the other hand, supported cooperation because of a middle-class hope of becoming entrepreneurs.[47]

Here one may discern the key to Ely's support for the Order, since it not only officially stood for cooperation but, also, for traditional middle-class values which Ely held so dear. Yet, what these events meant was that by 1886 the social situation in the United States had developed in such a fashion as to indicate to the Knights' working-class adherents that an organization with such abstract principles, and such a heterogeneous membership, could not effectively represent their interests in a steady manner. That is, the Knights, as evidenced by its handling of strikes, seemed to be too amorphous and unwieldy to represent effectively the growing militancy of a disgruntled working class. Foner relates the Knights' deterioration in the following manner:

> Already in 1885 and in 1886 the working class Knights were complaining of the ease with which non-working class elements joined the Order, and that it was more difficult for workers than owners of small businesses to join certain assemblies. . . . The chief complaint, however, was that non-working class elements were beginning to dominate the policies of the assemblies and direct them against the interests of the vast majority of the K. of L. membership. . . .
> It was evident in the winter and spring of 1887 during the bitter battle waged by 7,000 Knights in the Massachusetts shoe towns against an employers association lockout; again in September, 1887, during the strike of 60,000 Knights on the Reading railroad, and again during the strike of K. of L. workers at Braddock, Pennsylvania, in April, 1888. In each case . . . the General Executive Board refused to answer the appeals of the hard pressed strikers for funds. . . . In each case . . . [the board] urged the strikers to abandon the struggle, to oust the "radical elements" whom they blamed for the workers' difficulties, and to assure the employers that henceforth they planned to live in peace and harmony with capital.[48]

Based upon the evidence, it is warranted to maintain that the working class, in general, appeared to lose interest in the

Knights. Also, workers began to direct themselves away from middle-class cooperativist programs and to move toward a more channelized militancy premised upon economic organization with the strike as its ultimate weapon. Furthermore, the working-class contingent of the Order's membership tended to be concentrated in the larger cities and, as the overall membership of the Knights fell, so did the proportion of its members coming from the urban centers. Thus, whereas the Knights' membership stood at 7,000,000 in 1886, it was only slightly above 5,000,000 in 1887, less than 260,000 in 1888, and but 100,000 in 1890. In terms of the total membership, the proportion coming from large cities was about 44 percent in 1886, and dropped to 31 percent in 1888. These factors are particularly significant because a close alliance between the Order and farmer's organizations developed after 1889, while there was a simultaneous growth of the AFL in the larger cities.[49]

In one sense the Order of Knights of Labor and its cooperativist programs, along with its no-strike policy and loose membership standards, was based upon an insecure and shifting foundation. As one analyst put the matter, "its failure goes far to show that the union problem cannot be solved by any attempt to bring together in one organization the employing and working elements . . . unionism as a social problem must be accepted as an organization of wageworkers seeking their own interests as such."[50] Thus, the growing conflict between capital and labor continued and apparently could not be resolved through the cooperation of the classes in society founded upon Christian ethics or morality.

For Ely who, it has been said, "viewed himself as something of an intellectual aristocrat who should lead and direct from above the social order in the interest of all," it was no longer possible to maintain that the interests of all groups and classes in society were immediately compatible.[51] It seemed that one could no longer deign to speak for all, but rather would be forced by historical circumstance to choose from among the competing interests to determine where to lend one's voice.

Ely did not seem to have a difficult decision. When the Knights presented a social order with principles essentially similar to his own, Ely maintained that they were building

upon "true, scientific principles."[52] They represented the seed
within the old society from which a new cooperative order
would emerge. Since the trade unions did not provide a place
for employers and other elements, Ely had little hope for their
providing an impetus to the evolution of society toward the
ethical ideal of brotherhood.[53]

Since unions were lacking in this regard they were judged
inadequate and too narrowly based to stand for a general principle. In short, the trades unions were viewed no longer as a
universal panacea but, rather, as a particular interest within society. As such, one could no longer accept their cause as inherently beneficial; the conflict between capital and labor no longer appeared to possess an automatic solution. Labor demands
had to be measured against the now independently conceived
"social good." This "good" was, for all intents and purposes,
the ideals of traditional middle-class America. That ideal held
to the notion of a society as a system of checks and counter-
vailing forces as represented in a balance of social groups. That
balance, however, had its "pivot and stabilizer" in the existence
of a strong, independent middle class. In that sense, anything
that jeopardized that stabilizer threatened the entire social
good.[54] As Ely considered the matter:

> They [trades unions] are as a rule based on strife. They
> aim to prepare their members for industrial war. Now we
> must hope for peace in society, and an organization which
> does not look beyond contention to a cessation of strife
> has inherent in it a certain weakness . . . they have not
> been sufficiently interested in public measures and in re-
> forms designed to benefit society as a whole.[55]

After the eclipse of the Knights, and presented with no other
alternatives, Ely altered his views and came to insist that reform
must not come from the laboring class but, instead, from the
"superior" classes; that is, those with talent and an understanding of ethics.[56] In an article written in 1894, he condemned all
labor strikes as essentially detrimental to the public welfare and
applauded the use of the injunction in the Pullman dispute.[57]
As noted earlier, Ely's antilabor pronouncements began the

same year that he was brought before the board of regents at the University of Wisconsin. It would appear that for Ely the labor movement as such, now that the Knights had crumbled as quickly as they had arisen, was to share the villain role along with the ideologues of an unfettered laissez-faire. For Ely, then, the choice to be made was between two extremes—that of competition and that of socialism.

The implicit alliance that existed between the workers and the middle class within the Knights vanished when the Order collapsed and Ely's faith in labor was crushed. A turning point in Ely's conception of labor and reform, however, arrived after his reading of Henry Carter Adams's "The Relation of the State to Industrial Action."[58] Still, for a moment Ely appeared to stand alone, bereft of allies. Yet, in the twilight of the era one group calling for an end to conflict and the arrival of stability was the financiers and the large-scale industrialists who arrived upon the scene in the 1880s. In short, the teachings of Ely seemed now partially to complement the newly developed needs of the so-called financial capitalists. Ely himself appeared to recognize this.

In part, this recognition evolved from Ely's call for the institution of his own peculiar brand of socialistlike or cooperativist society. In this regard, Ely attempted to combine his early ideas on the moral society with the newer concepts propounded by Henry Carter Adams. Thus, Ely's later concept of "vested interests" appeared to be derived from Adams's ideas on proprietary rights in industry; still, Ely remained committed to the old belief in a cooperativist society.[59] For example, though he believed that the State as an ethical agency could own the means of production, the primary reason for its assuming such responsibilities now became that of reducing waste and increasing the amount of useful production. In that sense, the expanding industrial trusts seemed to represent a move in the right direction. What is more, Ely refused to countenance any form of an egalitarian distribution system in that he believed social rewards should be provided only to those with superior managerial skills.[60] Here, then, Ely stood by the traditional values of individual ambition and responsibility. It was for this reason that Ely's belief in the eventual evolution toward a cooperative social organization did not necessarily bring him into conflict with the great industrialists of the day. Though they might cause certain problems, Ely's old evolutionary scheme assumed they would eventually pass from the scene.

Ely's call for a cooperativist society, then, did not threaten the established order in America in that it was a visionary or utopian plan for the future. In fact, it implicitly defended the then contemporary social conditions to the extent that it relied on the existing elite to bring about the future moral state. Since this elite of "superior managerial skill" was necessary, the social conditions that supported it could not be condemned too harshly.[61]

When, after 1900, Ely did speak to the concrete policies of the present, he did not offer any ideas that departed very much from those first enumerated by Henry Carter Adams. While Richard Ely retained his moralistic philosophy even after the demise of the Knights of Labor, he rejected his earlier positive estimation of the labor movement in America. In essence, Ely's philosophy remained compatible with an affirmative attitude regarding labor only to the extent that the latter did not evidence tendencies toward socialism. Once such tendencies became apparent, the labor movement in the United States was transformed from a solution into a problem.

One now had to choose which particular social interest was more worthy of advocacy. Richard Ely presented his choice in the following manner:

> We may lay it down as a general principle . . . that as private property is a social institution it finds its limitations in the welfare of society. As soon as any of its forms or extensions become anti-social these should be suppressed. Private property is in general specially beneficial. . . . The disadvantages of private property appears in distribution, although here its effects are partially beneficial.[62]

One may say, then, that Ely's choice was on the side of the middle-class ideal of private property. The potential perfectibility of man was transformed into the potential perfectibility

of the capitalist system as a place where the middle-class belief
in initiative and success might rest secure.

While Ely did not find it difficult to express his choice between labor and capital in America, his philosophy did not provide any concrete suggestions for coming to terms with the
dilemma once the Knights of Labor passed from the scene. In
effect, Ely could only condemn militant labor because it threatened his philosophical ideal of the social good.

For this reason the later ideas of Ely were somewhat compatible with the interests of the trusts and the big industrialists.
Both big business and the traditional middle class were joined
in their defense of property against the rumblings of a militant
labor movement. However, the compatibility between Ely and
business could not be complete for two reasons. First, on theoretical grounds, Ely's ideas remained connected to a commitment to a cooperativist society. Ely's considerations of labor
up until 1894 had consistently criticized the nature of American society. In addition, his antilabor stand after 1894 could
be considered in some quarters as a revision and obtained under duress.[63]

In sum, then, Richard Ely rendered the analysis of the labor
movement as an acceptable topic and problem for political
economy. Yet, aside from his visions for the future, Ely was
unable to provide any solutions toward that problem. In fact,
the ideas of Henry Carter Adams originally brought about a
rethinking on the part of Ely, and it was Adams who first attempted to formulate a practical solution to the labor problem. It is to Henry Carter Adams that attention will now be
directed.

5 The Social Situation Confronting — Henry Carter Adams

A TURNING POINT IN RICHARD ELY'S thinking on the labor movement came after his exposure to the novel ideas of Henry Carter Adams, as indicated in the preceding chapter. In one sense, Adams replaced Ely as the primary intellectual force within the movement for a new political economy. Though it was Ely who was most responsible for instituting the new approach to economics in America and the first to address the problem of labor, it was Henry Adams who became the first to offer a concrete solution to that problem.

Born in Davenport, Iowa, in 1851, Adams's upbringing and early surroundings were similar to what Ely experienced.[1] Henry Adams, too, studied for the ministry but later changed his mind.[2] However, in terms of educational backgrounds, one may immediately discern a great deal of difference between the two men. Whereas Ely came to the study of political economy via an interest in philosophy and became familiar with economics only during his studies in Germany, Adams maintained an interest in economics throughout his student career.

In 1878 Henry Adams received the first doctorate to be granted by Johns Hopkins University. Thereupon, he set out for Europe to hear more of the new approach to economics. While in Germany he came under the influence of Adolph Wagner at Berlin, Adolf Held at Bonn, and Ernst Engel, the chief of the Prussian Statistical Bureau.[3]

When Adams returned to the United States in 1879 he was more convinced than ever that economics should not be left to the operation of free market forces as advocated by the English laissez-faire political economists. Instead, he argued for the in-

tervention of the State in the economy through the institution
of legal regulation. Such advanced views of a new economics
proponent was the reason for his eventual dismissal from Cornell University in 1887.[4] Fortunately, however, Adams was
able to secure an appointment at the University of Michigan
and remained there until his death in 1921. Adams also devoted much effort to governmental and administrative work. After 1900 most of his energies went into these channels. Among
his other activities, Adams was a statistician for the Interstate
Commerce Commission from 1887 to 1911; he assisted the
Michigan Tax Commission in the valuation of that state's railroads, and served as an adviser to the Chinese Republic for the
standardization of railroad accounts.[5]

It would thus appear that Adams's educational history was
somewhat more stable, and yet varied compared with that of
Ely in that an interest and familiarity in many areas of political
economy was sustained throughout his period of training and
beyond. It should be recalled that Ely's exposure to the new
economics was rather abrupt; his first experience occurred during his trip to Europe. Ely apparently underwent a conversion
experience during his travels as he came to accept completely
the new teachings he discovered in Germany. The effect of this
was reflected in his absolutist opinions regarding the moralistic
nature of the labor movement and the aims of the new economics. Such opinions were not held by Henry Adams. While not
enamored with the philosophy of laissez-faire, he learned its
principles early and was not prepared to discount them in toto.
That is, he attempted to strike a balance between English laissez-
faire political economy with its static, individualistic bias, and
the collectivism and historicism of the German economists.

In one sense, Adams was more balanced and selective in his
acceptance of the German historical approach. He was not certain that the German approach contained the solution to all
contemporary problems. One may see the differences between
Ely and Adams in their considerations regarding the worth of
the new economics as exemplified in the program of the American Economics Association, an organization they both helped
to found in 1885.

Both Adams and Ely saw the American Economics Association (AEA) as an organization that would offer an analysis of economic and social problems from a position which might serve as an alternative to laissez-faire. However, they tended to disagree on the manner in which this alternative was to be offered. Ely demanded the complete repudiation of laissez-faire and the exclusion of all orthodox economists from membership. In addition, he declared the major interest of the new economics to be in the area of social ethics. He therefore expected the involvement of the Church since, to him, the work of the AEA lay in the area of "practical Christianity."[6] In short, the AEA was to be the organizational expression of his moral program; it was to be an agency of immediate reform.

With Adams, on the other hand, the AEA was not to be an agency of advocacy but, rather, a scholarly organization whose aim was to facilitate the scientific analysis of economic problems. Thus, both proponents of laissez-faire and the new economics were permitted within its ranks. Most importantly, the organization was not to be committed to any political position. In fact, Adams felt so strongly on this matter that he refused to endorse Ely for the presidency of the economics group. Adams surmised that Ely's election would stand for the complete repudiation of laissez-faire which, in turn, might be construed as a virtual endorsement of the "German view of social relations" and the glorification of the state.[7]

Adams discountenanced such an impression for three reasons. First, he regarded Ely's collectivistic moralism as little better than a "knee-jerk" response to the excessive individualism of laissez-faire. Secondly, such an impression would make it extremely difficult to engage the support of the business community for any measures addressed to the problem of capital and labor conflict.[8] In addition, what rendered Ely's approach so troublesome was that it did not really provide any concrete solution for the problem. Proponents of the new political economy recognized that laissez-faire policies exacerbated the social problems which confronted an industrializing nation by demanding the repression of labor organizations. What Adams may have discerned was that so, too, did Ely's later views on labor in that they simply denounced the new militant type of working-class union organizations as unnecessary impediments in the path of the truly moral society.[9] In that sense, Ely's later views appeared to recapitulate the errors of laissez-faire. This was particularly problematic now that labor was militant in its struggle against capital and, in fact, often flirted with socialism.

As demonstrated in the previous chapter, labor was moralistic in a utopian way, during the early 1880s when the Knights of Labor represented the bulk of organized working men. However, with the formation of the American Federation of Labor and the demise of the Knights, the organized workers embarked on a program that sought to maximize their interests against the capitalist system itself. It was with the increase in such militancy that Henry Adams was most concerned.

It is necessary, here, to provide substance for the term "labor militancy," since there is a widespread impression that the American labor movement was always guided by a rather narrow pragmatism; that is, that it was always concerned only with higher wages and greater benefits, and that more idealistic or general social interests were foreign to it. In short, there is a common impression (which serves as a tribute to the influence of the fully developed Commons-Wisconsin School) that American labor really never posed a direct threat to the system of capitalism. In fact, during the late nineteenth century, American labor did pose such a threat through its adherence to a socialist-inspired program. It was precisely this threat that served as the focus for the theoretical efforts of Henry Carter Adams. While it is true that such a threat was recognized earlier by Richard Ely, he believed the threat would eventually be obviated through historical evolution. Henry Adams did not believe that the labor problem would disappear, as it were, simply through the workings of history. To appreciate Adams's concern it is only necessary to recognize the developments that transpired within the labor movement itself.

As James Weinstein indicated, though socialism never characterized the labor movement in America in its entirety, its presence and influence within that movement was nevertheless real, and did not decline until after the nation entered the First World War. Furthermore, even then, socialist sympathies grew among the rank and file of the movement.[10] In fact, socialist strength in the organized labor movement was at its peak in the period between 1881 and 1924, the very same years that witnessed the development of early labor theory in America.[11]

Though many of the leaders of the craft unions spoke of such things as "pure and simple unionism," they did not share the moralistic outlook of the Knights of Labor, nor did they necessarily assume the structure of capitalist society to be permanent. Even that brand of unionism represented by the Cigarmakers, with its program of high dues and benefits, was not in either theoretical or practical conflict with the socialism of the International Workingmen's Association. This was true in that a strong trade union movement was viewed as an absolute necessity to the socialist program.[12]

Regarding the compatibility between the American unions and socialism, it is interesting to consider that Friedrich Engels sided with Samuel Gompers and the American Federation of Labor (AFL) in a dispute it had with the Socialist Labor Party in 1891. In his autobiography, Gompers related that he wrote to Engels, whom he regarded as a friend, in order to receive advice regarding the Federation's refusal to seat a member of the socialist group at an AFL convention.[13] Though Gompers never received a personal reply, Engels did correspond with Hermann Schluter, a socialist and a member of the Brewery Workers' Union in the United States. Said Engels to Schluter regarding this dispute:

> I see clearly enough that things are going downhill with the S.L.P. . . . . compared to whom the Fabians here [England]—likewise bourgeois—are radicals . . . nor do I understand the quarrel with Gompers. His Federation is, as far as I know, an association of trade unions. Hence they have the formal right to reject anyone coming as a representative of a labor organization that is not a trade union . . . it was beyond question that it [the S.L.P. rejection] had to come and I, for one, cannot blame Gompers for it.[14]

Obviously the early AFL was not viewed by Engels or members of the International Workingmen's Association as an enemy or opponent of the proletarian socialist movement. Neither was it so viewed by the organizers of the Federation. Adolph

Strasser and P. J. McGuire, the former an organizer for the Cigar makers, the latter for the Carpenters, were both members of socialist organizations and looked upon their organizational activi ty as part of an overall socialist program. Strasser, who at one time was a member of the International Workingmen's Association, took up the task of organizing the skilled workers in Amer ica. He was later joined by McGuire who, at the time, was a member of the radical Social Democratic Party. What made these efforts particularly meaningful was that F. A. Sorge and others simultaneously set out to organize the unskilled under the banner of the International Labor Union (ILU). A plan existed whereby the Sorge and Strasser groups would eventually merge. Such a plan was initiated when Strasser attended the ILU convention of 1879.[15]

In effect, then, we may detect a socialist inspiration for the organization of American workers in the 1880s. As indicated in the preceding chapter, this was not at all surprising in the sense that labor violence and conflict of the mid-1880s could accurately be described as a "social war," and "a frenzied ha tred of labour for capital was shown in every important strike."[16]

One may find sentiments similar to those of Strasser and McGuire in the thoughts of Samuel Gompers, president of the AFL since 1886. Gompers did not believe that the unskilled should not be organized, but simply that organizations such as the Knights of Labor were not the proper vehicle for doing so.[17] As one commentator put the matter:

> The most curious aspect of the conflict between the
> Knights and unionists was that it was the most radical
> elements of both . . . that took the initiative in attempt-
> ing to destroy the other organization. . . . In a sense it
> was a latter day battle between Lasalleans and Marxists.[18]

In the 1890s most of Gompers's ideas and his general outlook reflected the inspiration of Marxist principles and he went so far as to declare that the culmination of the class struggle would af fect the "abolition of classes based on possession of wealth and power."[19] Such a policy was reflected in Gompers's defense of the economic organization of workers along trade lines. As he put it at the 1892 AFL convention, "what the toilers need at this time is to answer the bitterness and vindictiveness of the oppressors with Organization."[20]

That Gompers's intention was socialistic appears beyond dispute when one considers a statement to French workers that was promulgated and forwarded in the preceding year, "Comrades, though oceans divide us, the same spirit and purpose prompts us to seek in organization the final emancipation of the Proletariat of the World."[21] Recognition of the militancy of Gompers and the AFL was not lacking in the international socialist community. On the occasion of the celebration of Engels's seventieth birthday, Wilheim Liebknecht, August Bebel, Eleanor Marx Aveling, and other socialist and labor leaders, paid tribute to the AFL for its part in advancing the international struggle for the eight-hour day.[22] Even in the mid-1890s, Gompers went so far as to predict that the American workingman would soon turn toward independent political action to advance his interests.[23]

Such labor militancy and solidarity was not only present in statements by Federation leaders such as Gompers but, in fact, was present in the everyday struggles of the working people. In 1892, for example, the AFL provided solid support for the New Orleans general strike which not only united skilled and unskilled but also brought together black and white. At the famous Homestead, Pennsylvania, steel strike both the skilled and unskilled joined together and, in effect, brought about the temporary formation of an industrial union.[24] This generally militant, often socialistic, outlook was reflected in the public statements of the Federation. In 1895 an article appeared in the *American Federationist*, official organ of the AFL, acknowledging the trend of events:

> The feeling of wage-earners, i.e., the vast majority of people is growing more favorable to socialism. The attitude of dislike and intolerance towards the idea is passing away. . . . The increasing power of great combinations of capital, and the increasing hopelessness of wage-earners . . . is rapidly bringing about this change of heart.[25]

It is pertinent to note here reasons for growing labor militancy. First, unlike earlier eras, the circumstances around the end of the nineteenth century made it clear to many concerned workers that there would be no returning to a preindustrial status system. Secondly, the "increasing hopelessness of wage-earners" reflected the fact that the already lessened status of the worker was threatened with further erosion.

The reasons for this threat were not difficult to apprehend. For one thing, near the turn of the century "the movement toward consolidating industry that had been in progress for ten years or more" was nearing its end.[26] This process of business consolidation reached a climax in 1897 to 1904 and was symbolized by the organization of the United States Steel Corporation by Elbert Gary and J. P. Morgan.[27] Accompanying this trend was the continual increase in the number of workers. In 1889 there were well over four million such persons, an increase of 55 percent over that in 1879. By 1889 there were over five million workers, a 25 percent increase above the preceding decade's level.[28]

What might also be noted is that not only did such developments as business consolidation and centralization constitute a threat to the worker but, in addition, constituted a threat to the traditional middle class. This was because, as a result of these trends, socialism might be expected to gain more adherents. With the consolidation of industry and business and the growth of socialism, the middle class feared that the traditional opportunities open to it were fast disappearing. The belief in individual initiative and success seemed somehow out of place in the world. The pattern and social repercussions of economic growth greatly reduced the possibility that the success ethic might be realized.[29] In short, during this period, the autonomy of the worker and the ideals of the middle class were consistently threatened and brought into question. It would appear that the image of socialism was the more threatening of the two in that it openly challenged traditional middle-class beliefs.

As the middle class perceived a threat to its autonomy, so it was precisely a threat to autonomy—the relative degree of freedom or independence of the worker in the work process and in society at large—which constituted a significant source of labor

militancy during the era. In one sense, worker protest and organization was not simply a demand for narrow economic concessions but, in addition, a struggle to establish or retain some
degree of autonomy vis-à-vis big business and capital. As suggested by David Montgomery, and as Alain Touraine stated,
"Workers' attitudes are not only determined by satisfaction or
dis-satisfaction, adjustment or mal-adjustment, integration or
anomie, but also by an effort towards, and a demand for freedom."[30]

In considering this struggle for autonomy or "demand for
freedom," it may be understood to evolve in the following
manner. The skilled worker, one whose capacities are essential to the work process, may possess a great deal of autonomy
vis-à-vis capital due to the very indispensability of the particular skill which he commands. In other words, the greater the
amount of skill a worker must bring to use in the work process,
the greater is his relative autonomy (the greater is the workers'
ability to determine the manner in which work is to proceed;
working conditions, etc.). This is especially likely if the technical means of production, in terms of the industrial development
of society as a whole, are relatively unsophisticated. When such
conditions prevail, the autonomy of the individual worker and
the working class as a whole seems secure.[31] This is true in regard to the latter case because the capitalist class cannot dis-
pense with a particular group of workers but, rather, is dependent upon that group for the skills it brings to the work process.
In other words, by virtue of their needed skills, that particular
group of workers cannot be replaced by, for example, recruits
from the common "industrial reserve army of labor." If capitalists are in this sense dependent upon labor, labor may be said
to possess a degree of autonomy.

Anything that obviates the dependence of capital upon the
skill of labor contains the potentiality of decreasing labor's autonomy and increasing that belonging to capital. The latter situation, most obviously, will occur in periods of high technical
innovation and the concomitant displacement and dilution of
skills which accompany it. One may understand that this de-
creases labor's autonomy in that, in such circumstances, the
workers' skills come to be absorbed by machinery, which is

introduced through the initiative of capitalists. When viewed in this light, whether the worker is to retain autonomy or not depends upon the decisions of capitalists to introduce innovations.

Consequent to the introduction of innovations, and since the worker possesses little productive skill, the capitalist may unilaterally dictate the immediate conditions of work (wages, hours, rules, and procedures of work). To the extent that a worker brings nothing more than his labor power to the work process (that is, to the extent that he is strictly a "proletarian" in Marx's sense) he is dependent relative to capital. The struggle for autonomy is thus the continual attempt to combat the increasing control of the work process by capital.[32] If this descriptive analysis is essentially correct, one would expect labor militancy to be associated with heavy threats to worker autonomy. Again, worker autonomy would be expected to be lessened during periods of high technological innovation and, subsequent to such periods, this fact would be reflected in the capitalists' unilateral ability to determine working conditions.

When viewed from a Marxian perspective, the struggle for autonomy may be judged as either "reactionary" or "progressive," depending upon the particular form which that struggle assumed. For example, a worker struggle for autonomy against capital which took the form of machine smashing or the prevention of the installation of technical innovations would be deemed reactionary. Obversely, such a struggle in the form of worker demands for the control of the production process via the institution of socialism would be deemed progressive.

Though worker militancy might take a reactionary or progressive form, either of which introduce problems for the capitalist system as a whole, it is the latter form of militancy which is most threatening to the values of the old middle class. The movement for socialism requires the abolition of all forms of capitalism per se. Reactionary worker militancy, on the other hand, may sometimes be allied with the old middle class in that it does not struggle against capitalism per se, but only against one of its forms. This reveals one underlying reason why Richard Ely could view the Knights of Labor with favor, while both he and Henry Adams expressed great wariness with regard to the early AFL.

In sum, then, one should expect worker militancy, as reflected in socialist sympathies, to be heightened during periods of threat to worker autonomy. One would further expect such threats to be heaviest among work groups that possess some skill and, therefore, in an obvious sense, have the most to lose. Such periods of threats to autonomy would tend to be characterized by high rates of technical innovation (and skill displacement and dilution), and the consequent attempt by capitalists to dictate unilaterally the conditions of work.

Evidence is available to support the above interpretation of the struggles of capital and labor in America. If one considers the frequency of strikes as reflecting the militancy of labor at any one particular period of time, it may be seen that the peak frequency of strikes tends to coincide with periods of economic prosperity or upturns in the business cycle. That is, strikes and the business cycle tend to be positively related. Alvin Hansen, in an analysis of strikes for the period of 1881-1919, found that the peak of strike activity, during long-term periods of rising prices, tended to occur in direct association with the business cycle.[33] Similarly, in an analysis of strike activity for the period of 1881-1937, John Griffin found that the troughs of strikes corresponded with depressions.[34]

Such findings may give rise to the interpretation of strikes as "economistic" or "pragmatic" adventures; that is, they may be taken to prove that unions are prone to strike with a higher frequency during periods of prosperity since they may maximize their economic benefits. Obversely, it may be held that strikes fall off during depressions since the falling profits of capitalists leave little room for labor to extract any increases. While such an interpretation seems sensible from today's perspective, it is not necessarily valid to infer that the motivations of strikers during 1885 to 1910 were the same as those of the strikers of today, especially when we recall the relationship between the demand for autonomy and the impact of technical innovations. That relationship becomes particularly salient if one comes to recognize that machine sales enjoy a boom period precisely during upturns in the business cycle. Such is especially true if business competition takes the form of a struggle for a larger share in an expanding market and this, in fact, was the situation in American industry during the period under consideration.[35]

Thus, since both strikes and the application of technical innovations in industry tend to correlate with the business cycle, it is not valid to assume that the motivation to strike was purely economistic. It is also true that such strikes occurred because of the threats workers perceived against their autonomy. Again, one would expect such complaints to be the case in periods wherein technical industrial innovations could be described as excessive or unusually high.

However, the issue of autonomy versus economism in explaining trade union behavior is a controversial one. The relationship between contemporary strike activity and general business conditions remains in dispute. The situation can be only more clouded as one delves backward in time.

Since Hansen's study in 1921 there has been a plethora of research on the relationship between strikes and business conditions, but the data generated remain ambiguous. For example, in a 1953 article Levitt maintained that business prosperity may reduce, rather than encourage, strike activity.[36] But almost a generation later research by Jack Skeels failed to confirm the Levitt findings and, instead, upheld the more generally accepted and traditional economism thesis.[37] Yet, as early as 1940 the work of Yoder had cast doubt upon economistic explanations for the behavior of unions. After reviewing strike data for the 1880 to 1936 period, Yoder wrote, "while business conditions are reflected in strikes, there is no simple pattern of covariation . . . it is apparent that no significant covariation in month-to-month or year-to-year fluctuations can be depended upon."[38]

One reason for the lack of linear correlation between strikes and business conditions may be due to the impact of the autonomy issue for some workers at certain moments in the history of a nation's industrial development. This notion emerged clearly in the 1950s with the work of Reinhard Bendix.

In the period from 1880 to 1910 the United States underwent the most rapid economic expansion of any industri-

alized country for a comparable period of time. . . . This
speed of economic expansion was reflected in the ruthless
practices of American business leaders in the strident ide-
ologies espoused during this time. In England measures of
social reform and the organization of workers in trade
unions were well under way in the 1860's and 1870's. In
the United States, workers began to organize only in the
1890's.[39]

Research by David Montgomery revealed that there was a
significant occurrence of "control struggles" by American
workers in the pre-World War I era. That is, strikes occurred
to enable workers to maintain or establish control over conditions of work and often embodied the demand for union
recognition.[40] Recently Richard Edwards has argued for the
provision of greater attention to the autonomy issue for American workers between 1880 and 1920:

> Given this emphasis on events external to the sphere of
> production (e.g., prices, general business conditions,
> etc.), later commentators have been able to uncover on-
> ly the most general linkages between the increasing cen-
> tralization of production and the growth of the labor
> militance. . . . For bosses and workers, the transition
> brought an immediate change in daily life. That change
> occurred in capitalism's 'hidden abode', in the private
> sphere behind the doors marked 'employees only'. Here,
> the centralization of capital created a general crisis of
> control within the firm.[41]

For Edwards, then, the full meaning of early strike activity
may be discerned only insofar as it is considered in conjunction
with the issue of autonomy or "control within the firm" that
emerged between 1880 and 1920. Edwards suggests that attempts to explain trade union actions by general business conditions alone may be misleading. This suggestion found an echo
in the work of David Snyder who claimed that purely economistic explanations for early union behavior were premised on

rather dubious assumptions: "Where union membership is large and relatively stable, the political position of labor firmly established and collective bargaining well institutionalized, assumptions underlying the economic models hold well."[42] Yet, the assumptions necessary to support purely economistic explanations of union behavior in the United States were not valid until after World War II. Thus, the rapid trend toward centralization in industry and increased threats of technological innovation and unilateral control at the point of production could be expected to increase the importance of the autonomy issue for the early American workers.

Such threatening conditions did, in fact, exist in the 1885 to 1910 period. During the 1880s the role of the machine grew in importance to such an extent that during the decade the amount of horsepower employed in manufacturing establishments increased by 85 percent.[43] As Samuel Gompers was to comment in 1887, "The displacement of labor by machinery in the past few years has exceeded that of any like period in our history."[44] As one labor historian described the era:

> The eighties were years of marvelous industrial expansion. . . . The dominant feature was the introduction of machinery upon an unprecedented scale. Indeed, the factory system of production, for the first time . . . led to an increase in the class of unskilled and semi-skilled labour, with inferior bargaining power.[45]

When all these factors are recognized it becomes clear that the era epitomized the process that Schumpeter identified as one of "creative destruction." The hallmark of an expanding capitalism consists of the introduction of new methods of production, new markets, and new industrial organizations (such as trusts and combinations).[46] In fact, the twenty years from 1873 to 1893 witnessed the most rapid application of modern machinery that had occurred, to that time, in human experience.[47]

It is distinctly the case, then, that labor conflict during the period was motivated, at least in part, by the issue of worker autonomy. What must be clarified, however, is whether or not this struggle assumed an anticapitalist and prosocialist nature. That is, it must be demonstrated that the historical presentation of the autonomy issue was conducive to the development of prosocialist sentiments among the American workers.

Although it is extremely difficult to demonstrate that threats to autonomy gave rise to prosocialist sentiments among workers in any direct manner, there are indirect indications that such was the case; for example, a prosocialist resolution was introduced at the AFL convention of 1893. By examining the degree of support that the resolution received, the groups which supported it, and the situation of those groups, one may indirectly test the proposition that threats to worker autonomy were related to the rise of socialist sympathies among the workers.

During the course of the 1893 AFL convention, a socialist from Chicago introduced a resolution calling for the initiation of a political program which included a demand for "the collective ownership by the people of all means of production and distribution" (see Appendix 1). The proposal to submit the resolution to a membership vote was approved by the overwhelming margin of 2,244 to 67.[48] If a listing of those affiliated unions which unconditionally endorsed the motion to submit the political program to the membership is consulted, one finds the following groups to be included: United Mine Workers, Amalgamated Iron and Steel Workers, the Lasters, Tailors, Woodworkers, Flint Glassworkers, Brewery Workers, Painters, Furniture Workers, Street-Railway Employees, Waiters, Shoe Workers, Textile Workers, Mule Spinners, Machinists, and the German-American Typographical Union.[49]

When concern is addressed to the extent to which these groups faced the issue of autonomy, one finds that the following was the situation for union members. Considering the degree of technical innovation as revealed by the extent to which physical power is displaced by machinery (in the twenty-year period ending in 1886), it is the case that such displacement for shoe workers ran as high as 80 percent; for furniture workers, displacement ran at about 30 percent; and for some types of woodworkers, the rate was from 30 to 50 percent.[50] When attention is directed to the typographers one discovers that the

linotype machine emerged in the late 1880s with a large potential power of displacement. During the mid-1890s, the actual
amount of displacement of hand compositors was heavy.[51]

When one begins to consider the mine workers, it is revealed
that, in 1893, they faced large-scale wage cuts dictated by the
owners and experienced a great many hard-fought strikes. It
was only in 1890 that the workers were able to establish a
union in the face of discharges, blacklistings, and evictions carried out by company guards. In short, the miners were a particularly hard-pressed lot. Such was manifested in 1894 when they
engaged in a general strike which met with complete failure.[52]
The mine workers were virtually without any independence
vis-à-vis the mine owners.

Upon considering the machinists, one discovers that though
they were already unionized in 1888, by the 1890s they began
to lose their craft status due to the introduction of power machinery which permitted unskilled workers to replace them. As
John Laslett indicated, the machinist came to consider that he
"could never hope to improve his condition so long as the machine, the great leveller, remained in private hands."[53]

The brewery workers represent a somewhat more complicat-
ed group in that their socialism is traceable, in part, to the large
proportion of German immigrants among the union's leadership
and rank and file. However, it is also true that the brewers
worked under poor conditions and were experiencing a decline
in the craft nature of their occupation. Thus, aside from the
Germanic background of many brewers, the trade was characterized by bad conditions, low wages, and destruction of the
workers' skill components which were necessary to the brew-
ing process.[54]

One sees a similar situation among the tailoring trades. Prior
to 1900, not only were most persons in the trade unrepresented
by unions, but very often they worked under sweatshop conditions; the work rules therein were unilaterally dictated by the
shop owners.[55] An analogous condition was to be found among
the iron and steel workers after the famous Homestead strike of
1892. Not only was that strike a particularly brutal one in which
the Carnegie Steel Company employed virtually every imagin-
able tactic to crush the workers but, furthermore, the steel own-

ers were able to remove the union from the industry in such a way so as to forestall unionization for over a generation.[56]

Finally, regarding the situation of the textile workers, it is a well-known fact that since the beginning of industrialization, the textile trades were one of the heaviest centers of technical machine applications. Until the mid-1880s, the textile industry was often chosen to epitomize the modern industrial production system. The situation was such in the industry that socialists came to power within the National Union of Textile Workers within three years of its founding in 1891.[57]

A summary of the conditions which these preceding groups of workers confronted, along with the support which was given the socialist Plank 10 proposal at the AFL convention, may be seen in Table 3.

TABLE 3
Unions Favoring Submission of Plank 10 and the Autonomy Issue

Number of Unions for Plank 10	Unions Facing Recent Technical Innovations	Unions Where Capital Dictated Working Conditions	Unions for Plank 10 & Losing Autonomy
16	7	4	11
	(44%)	(25%)	(69%)

Source: John Commons and associates, *History of Labour in the United States,* vol. 2 (New York, 1918).

Thus, when the situation of those unions which supported submission of the prosocialist resolution at the AFL convention is considered, one finds that over two-thirds experienced threats to the autonomy of their memberships. Such threats were either in the form of heavy technological displacement or that of the unilateral determination of work conditions on the part of capital. Available evidence, then, suggests that the autonomy issue was related to the militant, prosocialist sentiments of AFL members at the end of the nineteenth century.

How significant was the autonomy issue in generating militant, prosocialist sympathies at the AFL convention? The data provided to this point provide no indication. However, a gauge of the significance of the autonomy issue may be obtained by considering further developments at the 1893 convention.[58] In arguments over the socialist program a motion was made to delete the phrase "for favorable consideration" from Plank 11 (for the entire socialist program, see Appendix). If it is assumed that those unions voting to retain the phrase were prosocialist in contrast to those voting to delete the phrase, then the significance of the relationship between the autonomy issue and socialist sympathies may be measured.[59]

In Table 4 the association between the autonomy issue and a "favorable" (prosocialist) vote on Plank 11 by union delegation is measured. A vote to delete the phrase containing the favorable instruction is interpreted to be "not favorable" (antisocialist). Unions wherein the delegation was divided evenly on the issue were considered as "split." The measure of association employed is the lambda statistic (λ) so as to predict prosocialist sympathies from a knowledge of the presence or absence of the autonomy issue.

TABLE 4
Autonomy Issue and Plank 11 by Union Delegation

		Present	Absent
Union	favorable	16	3
Delegation	split	2	0
Vote	not favorable	5	5
		$\lambda = 0.33$	
		$X^2 = 5.09, p. < 0.10$	

Source: American Federation of Labor Convention
Proceedings (Washington D.C., 1893).

Table 4 suggests that the knowledge of union status with regard to the autonomy issue permits one to reduce the error in predicting the attitudes of a union delegation toward socialism by one-third ($\lambda = 0.33$). The statistical significance of the data in Table 4, however, is not appreciable as is revealed by the value of chi-square ($X^2 = 5.09$).

In Table 5 the relationship between "favorable" (prosocialism) and "not favorable" (antisocialism) attitudes toward Plank 11 and the autonomy issue is considered by individual delegate votes. By virtue of this procedure no split votes may appear in the data. The lambda statistic (λ) is applied to measure the association.[60]

TABLE 5
Autonomy Issue and Plank 11 by Individual Delegate Vote

		Present	Absent
Individual	favorable	23	6
Delegate Vote	not favorable	10	13
		$\lambda = 0.30$	
		$X^2 = 6.99$, p.<0.01	

Source: American Federation of Labor Convention
        Proceedings (Washington, D.C., 1893).

The data in Table 5 reveal that knowledge of the status of the autonomy issue for a union provides one with almost a one-third reduction in error when predicting the vote of an individual delegate on Plank 11 ($\lambda=0.30$). The likelihood that the distribution of votes found in Table 5 is due to chance is negligible as is suggested by the value of chi-square ($X^2 = 6.99$).

Tables 4 and 5, together, suggest that the autonomy issue had a significant association with the occurrence of militant and prosocialist sympathies within American labor. Obviously the autonomy issue alone does not explain all things relevant to the appearance of militant and prosocialist attitudes among AFL affiliates. The point here is simply that the autonomy issue provides an important element which is necessary to understand fully the behavior of pre-World War I workers. Furthermore, in that the data are derived from the situations faced by workers in 1893, it is probable that the strength and importance of the association between the autonomy issue and prosocialist sympathies is understated. As David Montgomery noted, struggles for autonomy ("control struggles" in his terminology) actually were more prominent after the turn of the century, especially

during 1901 to 1904 and 1916 to 1920.[61] In short, threats to
American workers as expressed by the autonomy issue increased during the first two decades of the twentieth century.

Also, of note is that this threatening situation was exacerbated by the great influx of immigrants that poured into America during the final decade of the 1800s. As Foster Dulles observed:

> . . . the increasing introduction of labor-saving machinery
> on the one hand, and the rising tide of immigration on
> the other, interrelated to maintain a constant surplus of
> labor. Not only did this situation hold down wages, but
> it heightened the feeling of insecurity among workers.[62]

If the autonomy issue provides a key to an understanding of
the militant nature of the American labor movement from
1885 to 1910, one should expect that when that issue was no
longer manifest labor militancy would decline. That is, as the
threat of technological displacement of the workers' skill diminished and, or, large-scale capital did not insist upon the unilateral determination of working conditions, one would expect
labor militancy to decrease. The first is likely—the lessening of
the technological threat—once capital has developed to such an
extent that a significant degree of trustification already exists.
This is true, in that, to the residue of skilled workers who sur-
vived the preceding waves of innovation, the wide-ranging machine applications are something in the past and technology
poses less of an immediate threat. In short, in view of the mas-
sive innovations of the past, current technical improvements
seem slight and the basis of the workers' skill appears secure.
The second is likely—no insistence upon the unilateral determination of work conditions—if the skill levels of craft workers remain high enough to render them indispensable to capital
in the work process. The probability that such will occur, then,
depends upon that power a trade or craft possesses due to its
indispensability.

What must be noted, however, is that other reasons may exist for the restraint of organized capital. These may be summar-
ily considered as reasons of public relations, that is, to foster a

favorable image with the larger public. This restraint seems to be more likely the more recent is the date of business centralization. In short, new forms of business organization may seek to indicate that they are deserving of legitimacy, displaying a benevolent attitude is one manner of securing such approval.

As long as skill components represent a relatively small contribution to the work process, the power that may arise there tends to be diminished in that such represents, in one sense, an anomaly which stands against a high organic composition of capital. That is, skilled workers represent a fairly small portion of all workers whose amassed strength is inconsequential when compared to the resources of capital. This is especially true of "trustified" or monopolistic industries where competitive demands do not necessitate an emphasis upon uninterrupted production. On the other hand, the indispensability of a skill is magnified if a firm is in a competitive situation in that, since a skill is scarce, it is difficult to replace on short notice. The power of a trade or craft, then, is very real in the latter situation. This may be considered as giving rise to an economic reason for the restraint of capital.

What is significant, however, is that to the skilled workers in monopolistic industries, cause and effect can appear reversed and restraint on the part of big business may be assumed to be the result of the power of labor. As indicated, the autonomy and power of labor is real only in competitive industries; in monopolistic industries it is only apparent. One may come to understand the feelings on the part of union members when the conclusions presented by George Barnett to an early study of the impact of innovations upon American unions are considered:

> When machinery is first introduced, the line between
> those displaced from the trade and the survivors has
> not yet been drawn. Every member of the union is po-
> tentially a displaced workman. The only policy, there-
> fore, which fulfills the hope of every member is that of
> completely stopping the progress of the machine. . . .
> [But experience has shown that] at any given moment
> the union is interested in displacement from the trade as

it reacts upon the working conditions of the skilled men
still employed in the trade. It is not, therefore, the avoid-
ance of displacement of skill from the trade which forms
the primary concern of the union, but that partial displacement of skill characterized by lower wages and longer
hours for the handworkers.[63]

Thus, to the extent that work conditions are not substantially altered consequent to the introduction of machinery, it may
appear to the workers who remain that their positions are secure because of the necessary nature of their remaining skills.
If this is the case, threats to worker autonomy will not be perceived as very great. Once these points are understood it is no
surprise to discover that during the era of "trustification"
(around 1900), the tide of labor militancy was able to maintain itself in the monopolized industries while it gave way to
conservative or economistic unionism in competitive industries which employed skilled labor. For example, trade agreements did not exist between labor and capital in any of the industrial trusts, and it was such collective agreements which
were the hallmark of economistic unionism. The policy of instituting trade agreements was advocated by the National Civic
Federation (NCF), a private group bringing together both labor
and capital in the interest of reconciliation.

If one considers those union officers who supported association with the NCF one finds them to have been the leaders of
the Railroad Brotherhoods, Iron, Steel and Tin Workers, Gran-
ite Cutters, Longshoremen, Machinists, Iron Molders, Printers,
Carpenters, bricklayers, Street-Railway Employees, Boot and
Shoe Workers, Bottle Blowers, and Textile Workers.[64] None of
these unions were represented in any of the so-called greater
industrial trusts, which were composed of the following companies:[65]

Amalgamated Copper

American Smelting and Refining

American Sugar Refining

Consolidated Tobacco

International Mercantile Marine

Standard Oil

United States Steel

As Perlman indicated, "On the whole trade unionism held its own against employers in strictly competitive industries. Different, however, was the outcome in industries in which the number of employers had been reduced by monopolistic or semi-monopolistic mergers."[66] Yet, even those groups participating in the reconciliation programs of the NCF were not immune to the unilateral demands of big capital. In June, 1901, at the same time that the Machinists' Union and the National Metal Trades Association were cooperating in trades agreements through the NCF, the Association was breaking extant agreements it already had with the union. It was such occurrences which made the NCF appear ridiculous before the public.[67]

It cannot be denied that a conservative or economistic trend was present in the labor movement. Yet, such a trend tended to be representative of those labor groups with the characteristics enumerated earlier, groups of skilled workers employed in competitive industries. This was significant, however, in that the strongest and most stable unions, prior to World War I, were found in the transportation, building, printing, and coal mining industries.[68] All possessed the characteristics of skilled workmen in competitive industry and, save for the miners, tended to be conservative. Thus, those unions which controlled the largest contingent of votes at the AFL conventions tended also to be the most conservative. At a later date Samuel Gompers, the Federation's president, was to become more and more amenable to the views of those unionists.

During 1885 to 1910, then, it is clear that the American labor movement was home to two contrasting trends. In the 1890s the AFL was militant and tended to be anticapitalist and prosocialist. After approximately 1900, however, the skilled trades within competitive industries became more conservative or economistic. What must not be forgotten is that, in some cases, this conservatism depended to a large extent upon the acceptance of the idea of the trade agreement on the part of the large-scale capitalists. As was seen in the case of the Machinists, this acceptance could be withdrawn capriciously. This might also be seen in terms of the strike conducted by the Amalgamated Association of Iron and Steel Workers in 1901 against the United States Steel Corporation. While that corporation was in the process of formation, trade agreements did exist. However, once the company was effectively organized and public opinion gauged, the agreements were broken and the union destroyed.[69]

The two contrasting trends in the labor movement were united in terms of the autonomy issue. That is, threats to autonomy tended to produce militant workers while the absence of such tended to produce economism. However, since threats to autonomy were continually arising during this period, the plight of the Machinists and the Iron and Steel Workers may serve as examples, the presence of worker militancy was continuous and, in fact, growing.

That the fate which befell the Iron Workers was not rare may be judged from the fact that the era of trustification was characterized by some labor historians as a "honeymoon period of capital and labor."[70] Though unions entered into trade agreements with management due to a lessening of the perceived threat of displacement and an apparently changed attitude on the part of capital, such agreements were broken when business no longer had use for them. In short, the autonomy issue became latent during the time of monopoly formation. The large corporation, preoccupied with the details of consolidation and the floating of securities, along with the reaction of the public to such mergers, had no desire for clashes with labor.[71]

All this tended to be beyond the vision of many workers and the emergence of trade agreements was interpreted by them as an indication of labor strength. Yet, as these agreements were soon shattered, attitudes changed. According to one commentator, "Since 1900 socialism has been making rapid progress in the labor ranks. . . . It now commands about one-third of the votes at the convention of the American Federation of Labor."[72] One may understand the reasons for this, in that, while the early period of monopolization witnessed an upsurge in trade agreements it did not take long for the autonomy issue to again raise its head. It did so when big business decided unilaterally to break such agreements. The United States Commissioner of Labor conducted an exhaustive study of strikes from 1881 to 1905 and found that whereas the total number of strikes from 1893 to 1898 was 7,029, such numbers more than doubled to 15,463 in the years 1899 to 1904. Apparently, as American capitalist society matured the amount of labor protest increased. What is of particular significance, however, is the fact that not only did the number of strikes increase over time but, in addition, the nature of strikes was altered.

In 1881 three-fifths of all strikes were for increased wages and only one-sixteenth for union recognition. In short, most strikes were purely defensive and represented an attempt by the workers to remain in step with immediate economic conditions. When the strikes of 1881 are compared with the strikes of 1905 the differences are immediately salient. In 1905 only about one-third of the strikes were for wage increases, and somewhat more than 30 percent were for union recognition. What is of added interest is that whereas the unions were responsible for less than one-half of all strikes in 1881, they instigated nearly three-fourths of those in 1905.[73] Thus, union activities for the latter date are not simply more numerous but also more agressive and militant. As suggested earlier, this was associated with the workers' perceptions of threats to their autonomy.

It seems clear, then, that the situation Henry Carter Adams faced was one of a militant labor movement leaning toward socialism and thereby threatening the foundations of capitalist society. Given the social conditions enumerated in this chapter, these trends in labor could be expected to gather momentum. Chapter 6 analyzes the concern Adams directed toward this turn of events.

6 Henry Carter Adams Addresses the ___ Labor Problem _____

HENRY ADAMS ACCEPTED THE MILITANCY of the labor movement and its demands for autonomy as the central problem for political economy in the closing decade of the nineteenth century. Such an attitude followed from the fact that he looked upon the world of middle-class, nineteenth-century America as a "true democracy" and, therefore, worthy of preservation. For him socialism was to be avoided and, thus, socialistic developments within the labor movement were to be countered. As he expressed these sentiments in the *Princeton Review* in 1884:

> It has become quite fashionable to smile at the Declaration of Independence. . . . But such a smile indicates intellectual weakness rather than strength since it shows that one cares for words more than for the spirit of an age—or the truth of an idea so great that it moved a generation.[1]

Basically, Adams considered himself a conservative in that he wished to preserve such an ideal as described above. His primary motivation was clearly, and admittedly, antisocialist. Commenting in the essay, "The Relation of the State to Industrial Action," he related:

> The opinions expressed in this essay are motivated by the theory of individualism . . . they trace the evils of existing society to the fact that the principle of social powers has

Portions of this chapter appeared previously in *Journal of the History of Sociology* Vol. 1, No. 2 (Spring 1979).

been arrested in its development, and they look for escape from present difficulties to the extension of this principle in industrial affairs . . . its aim is to bring industrial society into harmony with the fundamental thought of our political constitution. There is no other escape from socialism.[2]

That Adams was aware of his own values and motivations is beyond doubt. He was committed to the values of the traditional middle class and desired to see them perpetuated; socialism, therefore, was to be combated. It is also apparent that the older principles of laissez-faire were to be opposed because they culminated in an "arrested development" of the idea of personal responsibility. That is, in effect, the principles of laissez-faire were rendered inoperable under contemporary social conditions. A way to realize those principles had to promulgated. The general system and outlook of English economics was not to be booted out, but simply revamped to fit present circumstances. Thus, while advocating a new economics, the intention was to preserve within it the essence of the old. In this sense, Adams appeared to employ the Hegelian concept of transcendence:

> No doctrine could have gained such a respectable following except if it contained some truth, and it is wise to search for that truth. . . . English economy lost its authority because it abandoned principles and took to presumptions. It can never regain its authority until it returns to principles. . . . This is the problem for the "new economy," and nothing but its solution can warrant the claim that a new economy has been born.[3]

Thus, Henry Adams was conservative in a wide, philosophical sense and in the somewhat narrower sense regarding the discipline of political economy, which rendered him a defender of the political-economic system. Accordingly, he was interested in preserving the viability of the system as a whole, and this served as the focus for his theoretical endeavors. In 1886 he wrote, "The energies of a growing and expanding society are

directed to the service of a favored class; and this, when it becomes generally apparent, gives rise to an unhealthy discontent
which checks further expansion."[4]

Clearly, then, Adams recognized the intentionality or value-
premise of his own position. What is more, however, he realized
that any serious attempt to come to terms with the labor problem would not arise from an effort which merely sought to protect or advance immediate interests. In other words, contemporary problems might only be solved through extensive study
and analysis. The scholar, aware of his own biases and values,
would be the one to undertake the task. Wrote Adams:

> The scholar differs from either the laborer or the states-
> man when contemplating modern society in that he is not
> retained to represent any particular interest. He views the
> movements of society as it were from a height.[5]

In effect, what Adams proposed was to remove himself from
the immediate interests of an extant social group in order to
grasp their more general interest; that is, to view the long-term
interest. The essential goal of this activity was to find a way to
rationalize or channel the growing labor militancy which threatened the system. In order to do so, one had first to engage in
scholarship and theory. In this regard Adams came to represent
and advance the ideal of traditional middle-class society—the
entrepreneurial businessman.

It is clear that Henry Carter Adams did not view the labor
movement as inherently moral as did the early Ely. Instead, the
militant labor movement was viewed as simply a fact of life, a
natural outcome of development within a laissez-faire capitalist
society. It was neither moral nor immoral but simply something
that had to be dealt with. An effective solution would prove to
depend on one's understanding of the causes of discontent.
This was, as indicated earlier, the goal of Adams's "new economy." The search for the causative element in the labor problem was the hallmark of Adams's approach. Only when that
element was grasped might the system survive the threat that
developed within it:

It is by no means universally admitted, even among the studious, that the power of government, which properly interpreted is but the authoritative will of society, should be more sparingly used as society becomes more complex. . . . It is certainly true that much of current legislation enfolds within itself the seeds of a "coming slavery." . . . But our escape from such pernicious consequences will not be found in the continued proclamation of a negative philosophy. The only scholarly course lies in subjecting social and industrial relations to a deeper analysis than is presented by those who submit superficial plans of reform . . . the collapse of faith in the sufficiency of the philosophy of laissez-faire, has left the present generation without principles adequate for the guidance of public affairs. . . . Principles of action we must have, for nothing is so mischievous as the attempted solution of great questions on the basis of immediate interests alone.[6]

As the laissez-faire economics, the negative philosophy, was inadequate for guiding contemporary social action, so, too, was the Germanic principle of Statism. That is, while laissez-faire dictated that no State interference should function in the economy, the Germanic principle dictated that the State should exercise great discretion in economic affairs.

Here, it may be recalled, the early ideas of Richard Ely advocated the complete acceptance of the labor movement through the implementation of governmental policy reforms. Where the government formerly acquiesced in permitting the unbridled rule of capital in the economic world, Ely demanded that the government come to unabashedly champion the cause of labor. While he no longer championed the cause of labor, Ely later expected the State to absorb eventually the function of production. Yet, until that time arrived, Ely's later ideas granted de facto hegemony to the large-scale industrial capitalists of the day. These were the ideas Adams was objecting to; he considered them to be just as superficial and unreflecting as was the defense of the English ideal of laissez-faire:

> The fundamental error of English political philosophy
> lies in regarding the state as a necessary evil; the funda-
> mental error of German political philosophy lies in its
> conception of the state as an organism complete within
> itself. Neither the one or the other of these views is cor-
> rect . . . the present is a critical epoch in the history of
> the American people. . . . It is a mistake to admit of any
> compromise between these ideas.[7]

Thus, both the English and German views were poor views
in Adams's opinion. Yet, he did not believe that all State action
was an evil, but only that which strove to be all-encompassing.
To Adams, State action in the economy was desirable but it
had to remain within certain bounds. As he commented in the
latter half of the 1880s (in apparent disagreement with the
views of Ely regarding the advent of a cooperativist society),
"It is an intellectual blunder to say that all extensions of government are in the direction of socialism, for it may be that
such a movement contemplates merely the extension of responsible control over a business which would otherwise be irrespon-
sibly managed."[8]

Here, it appears that "irresponsibility" is the term applied to
businesses which, in their singular attempt to realize their immediate interests, give rise to forces which directly undermine
the general conditions necessary for their existence. In this
view, then, the capitalist who simply maximizes his day-to-day
interests with no regard for the effect of such behavior upon
the capitalist system as a whole—the very structure which sup-
ports the framework within which his daily activity is conducted—is grossly irresponsible. In effect, capitalism must be checked lest it turn against itself.

It seems clear, then, that Adams's thought sought a course
somewhere between the policies of the English and the Germans.
When one seeks the reason for this view, caution must be exercised since some interpretations of Adams's attempt to find a
middle road portray him as an historicist who contended that
the cultural essence of different societies dictated which kind

of State action was viable. Mark Perlman expressed this vein of thought:

> Adams argued that every nation had its own unique historical measure for the degree of state intervention considered desirable . . . Adams noted that in America a third, or middle course, seemed to have developed [between the extremes of the German and English models].
> . . . He therefore sought a formula for the practical intervention of the state in America.[9]

This historicist reading of Adams does not appear to be accurate for two reasons. First, it assumes that the laws or tendencies within society are relative to each nation, and, secondly, that such relativity is determined by the unique nature of a particular nation. It suggests that the practical action within a nation must be compatible with its unique nature. One may clearly comprehend that such an interpretation of Adams's views is in error when his following statement is considered:

> Society is the organic entity about which all our reasoning should center. . . . Society, as a living and growing organism, is the ultimate thing disclosed by an analysis of human relations. . . . It is futile to expect sound principles for the guidance of intricate legislation so long as we overestimate either public [Germanic principles] or private [English principles] duties; the true principle must recognize society as a unity, subject only to the laws of its own development.[10]

One may understand, then, that for Adams the English and Germanic principles were unsatisfactory not because they were incompatible with the unique nature of American society but, rather, because they represented partial and, therefore, inadequate understandings of society as such. Inadequate understandings could never yield adequate courses of action. Such might only emerge from an understanding of the laws of social development.

Adams's search for a particular practical course of action did not connect with the supposed uniqueness of a nation; though action might vary within each nation, such variability was connected with the interests of groups within each nation. That is, variations in action were connected to variations in interests. Thus, for example, the Germanic view of State and society was not appropriate to America in that the German State had dictated the course of economic development due to the lack of a strong, indigenous bourgeoisie within that nation. On the other hand, the English principle of laissez-faire had emerged earlier from a powerful bourgeois interest. Yet, under contemporary circumstances laissez-faire, itself, gave rise to a militant wave of "new unionism" in Britain which threatened social stability.[11] In short, when society continued to operate closely along the lines of laissez-faire there emerged a militant labor movement. This was the very occurrence Adams was interested in curbing.

Thus, the ideas of Henry Adams were not historicist in the usual sense of the term. Rather, Adams appeared to believe in laws of social development (though not in an absolutist sense as was the case with the advocates of laissez-faire). The course of action which he would come to propose was not due to the unique nature of American society but, rather, to the specific interest he embraced—the stabilization and preservation of the middle-class ideal of the American political-economic system. The English view was inadequate because it tended to give rise to destabilizing phenomena; the German view was inadequate in that it did not offer policies in the interest of an independent middle class.

What must now be determined is the "true" or adequate principle which Adams viewed as a guide to an acceptable course of action in America. In order to do so it is necessary to understand his ideas on the causation of the labor militancy of the period. This, in effect, leads toward an understanding of his consideration of the nature of the labor movement. During the second strike against the Gould Railroad system in 1886, Adams offered such a consideration:

> The labor movement marked the attempt to achieve "industrial liberty" as the necessary complement to religious and political [liberties] . . . . Since the structure of modern

industry, based on machinery, required concentration of capital, it followed that laborers must unite or they would surely get the worst of the bargain. Underlying labor's demand was the idea that the laborer has some right of proprietorship in the industry to which they give their skill and time . . . that workingmen resort to violence and employers call for troops was the result of the fact that labor had nothing to lose under existing arrangements . . . [if demands for liberty are heeded] workmen would receive the benefits of industrial partnership without disturbing the existing nominal or legal ownership, and a new law of productive property would arise.[12]

At a later time, Adams expanded and explicated what he meant when he had indicated that the labor movement constituted a force moving toward the institution of "industrial liberty." In 1891 he delivered an address entitled, "An Interpretation of the Social Movements of Our Time," in which he indicated that

the worker has lost control over the conditions of labor, and the labor agitation of our own times, so fearful in its tendencies, so demoralizing in the bitterness of hatred engendered, is but the effort of workingmen to gain control over the conditions in which work shall be done. . . . A social philosophy adjusted to a scheme of domestic industry has been maintained, not withstanding the fact that domestic industry has given way to the factory system.[13]

During his presidential address to the American Economics Association in 1896, he further explicated his basic idea of the "job-right" or the workingman's "proprietary right":

The workmen are reckless because in the evolution of modern industry they have been bereft of all proprietary interest in the plant that gives them employment; the employers appeal to force because there is nothing else to which they can appeal for the restraint of propertyless men. . . . The truth is, the regime of contract can-

not work unless all men are in substantially the same condition concerning property; not . . . in the amount of
property held, but in the relation which proprietorship
establishes between the proprietor and industry. . . . The
development of juris-prudence that is needed, therefore,
does not pertain to fundamental principles. It must address itself rather to the clarification of those concepts
dimly present in all industrial controversies. It is a common law development and not a constitutional change,
or a statutory enactment, that is needed.

Adams was to conclude that "the sociology of the industrial
process has rendered collective bargaining imperative, in order
that due regard may be paid to the instinct of individualism by
which both [employer and employee] are impelled."[14]

What one may recognize here is that the workers' quest for
"industrial liberty," as Adams expressed it, is equivalent to the
demand for autonomy. So, Adams's ideas appear to agree with
those expressed in the preceding chapter to the effect that
worker militancy arose as a consequence of what workers perceived as threats to their autonomy. What is most significant is
the cause Henry Adams attributed for this development. For
him, the application of machinery and the concentration of
capital were of primary import in that they tended to render
the worker "bereft of any proprietary interest" and, in fact,
"propertyless." When the worker perceived this transformation
from proprietorship to propertylessness, or movement from a
position of independence toward one of dependence, he recognized the threat to his autonomy as it was manifest in the expansion and development of capital.

A significant point is the manner in which this transformation from property to propertylessness occurred. Adams indicated that "the worker has lost control over the conditions of
labor," and this was sufficient to understand the relative lack
of autonomy in the present epoch. However, dependence or
powerlessness is not synonymous with propertylessness, and
it was this latter phenomenon which Adams also implicated
as a cause for labor militancy. Yet, this is not, in actuality, a
different cause but, rather, a separate moment in the same

causal chain—the erosion of autonomy. That is, the loss of control over work process is a concomitant of the transformation from proprietorship to propertylessness.

Once the matter is understood in this fashion, one may recognize that the transition from "domestic industry" to the machine-based "factory system" played a most important role in this transformation. It was this very transition that witnessed the transformation of the worker from a skilled to an unskilled individual. Indeed, the movement of industry toward the factory system left the worker with nothing to sell but his labor power—a condition of virtual propertylessness. Whenever the worker possessed something over and above his labor power to be sold—that is, a skill—he was not in a condition of propertylessness but possessed a form of property in an amount varying with the degree of that skill.

The transition from proprietorship to propertylessness is the movement toward the factory system and the transformation of skilled into unskilled labor. The loss of worker autonomy or "industrial liberty" is, thus, not simply lost control over the conditions of labor but, furthermore, the loss or displacement of skills. In short, the possession of skill permits one to determine, in part, the conditions of work, while the loss of skill detracts from one's ability to determine such conditions. Technological innovations, under conditions of capitalist production, serve to undermine worker autonomy and thereby lessens worker control over the conditions of labor.[15]

What all this indicated, in effect, was that worker militancy was a consequence of the loss of autonomy and the loss of autonomy, in turn, could be traced to the elimination or displacement of the skills which the laborer formerly had brought to the production process. Adams was thus successful in isolating a causative element in the generation of labor militancy and anticapitalist sentiment.

By affording the worker a "proprietary interest" in industry —by giving him a job-right—Adams was convinced that worker protests could be managed within the framework of the extant political-economic system.[16] The reasoning for such was that collective bargaining, or the job-right, provided an artificial form of property in lieu of the real property of the worker's

skill. Any worker who possessed such job-rights in industry
would no longer be in a position of complete dependence vis-
à-vis capital. What must be considered, however, is the degree
to which such "rights" actually provided autonomy to labor
and whether or not such was the intention of the concept of
the job-right.

An answer to this query may be inferred from Adams's statement that when the existence of a favored class "becomes apparent, [it] gives rise to an unhealthy discontent which checks
further expansion."[17] That is, the specific problem was the impediment that was placed upon the continued viability of the
system, and the primary task was to remove that impediment.
As far as Adams was concerned, the institution of workers'
proprietary rights in industry was the manner by which discontent might be controlled and the method by which political
economy could demonstrate a return to principles:

> There is no reason in the nature of the case, why harmony
> cannot be restored to the industrial world, and why the
> science of Political Economy may not recover that sym-
> metry and form of which it has been deprived by the tren-
> chant criticisms of the last fifty years.[18]

Thus, the major problem, again, was to restore harmony to
the system and the agent of disharmony was already identified
by Adams—the recognized existence of a "favored class"—or,
in other words, a class that enjoyed privilege in contrast to one
that was dependent. It is significant that for Adams it was not
the existence, as such, of a favored class that was problematic
but, instead, the transparency of that existence. As he indicated
at a later date, "The cause of discontent lies in the minds of
men."[19]

Thus, one may understand that the problem could be resolved not only by obliterating the objective circumstances
that produced it but, as an alternative, by rendering such circumstances less obvious. In this sense the solution to the crisis
facing society did not demand a restriction upon the autonomy
of private business interests in a form that would necessitate the
decreased dependence of labor, but only in an apparent increase

in the autonomy of the worker. For Adams, this increase was to be brought about "by imposing upon labor the responsibility" which would go hand in hand with their new-found rights.[20]

Henry Carter Adams was cognizant of the process that brought about the dependency of labor vis-à-vis the autonomy of large-scale capital; namely, the transition to machine production and its absorption of the workers' skill, and it appears that he also recognized that labor would possess but a sense of autonomy through the institution of his idea of the job-right. Moreover, Adams regarded the capitalist as essentially a productive and valuable member of society, an attitude that was readily apparent in Adams's consideration of the operation of business by monopoly as contrasted to its operation by "talent." This latter characteristic seems to be specific to the ideal entrepreneur:

> Prices are determined by the ordinary or average cost of production, but if by superior business talent the cost of producing goods in a few establishments is less than the average, or if superior organization permits more work to be done . . . there is in this manner created an unusual margin between cost and price which gives rise to unusual profits . . . to state this distinction another way: a fortune built out of a monopoly is made up from the excess of the market price over the necessary cost of production, while a fortune created by business talent springs from depressing the cost of rendering a service below the average necessary price.[21]

In effect, Adams indicated that the monopolist (to the extent that he enjoyed high profits simply by forcing prices over costs) was a parasitic or non-productive agent. Such businesses Adams referred to as "industries of increasing returns" and he called for their public regulation.[22] Significantly, Adams was silent as to the various modes that existed for "depressing the cost of rendering a service below the average necessary price."

Clearly, if the businessman simply forced prices above his costs the business was to be regulated through the intervention of the State. Yet, what if he used an equal amount of force not

to increase prices but to depress costs below the average by instituting wage cuts or prolonging the working day without raising
wages proportionately? It appears that these were precisely the
types of contingencies Adams had in mind when he formed his
conception of the workers' job-right. Such policies would clearly display the power and autonomy of capital and the utter dependence of labor in an immediate and direct way. In short,
the unbalanced relationship between the two classes would be
immediate and transparent in such circumstances: labor protest, violence, and militancy would be expected to follow.

One is left, then, with the third case in which "business talent" is responsible for depressing costs below the average. The
most basic of such talents is the application of technical innovations to industry which thereby reduce the labor time necessary to produce a given quantity of goods and thus lower the
costs of production. In short, further machine refinements and
the introduction of new forms of machinery are a prime source
of lowering costs and thereby increasing the margin between
cost and average price. This constitutes the most basic threat
to the autonomy of the worker under industrial capitalism.
That is, as we have seen, to the extent that the worker is bereft
of skill he is bereft of property and, yet, Adams endorses the
very process which brings this condition about. What is more,
if the worker exercises a choice as to the immediate conditions
of his labor, as in collective bargaining, he possesses autonomy.
However, to the extent that the range and types of such choices
are constantly being revised and dictated by the machine—
which determines the control over and the nature of work—autonomy is only illusory or, at best, transitory. As long as one's
choices or range of influence are determined by another, one is
dependent in that the availability of choice itself, as well as the
content of that choice, is within the purview of another. In
short, the worker remains dependent upon the capitalist, while
the latter is autonomous; he provides and determines the
choices of the former.

This relationship of autonomy and dependence, once bargaining is instituted, is not immediate or readily apparent and,
as such, is unlikely to fuel the source of discontent, which
Adams located in the minds of men. What would be accom-

plished through Adams's proposal was that business would no longer be operating in an "irresponsible" fashion. It would no longer be permitted to undermine unconsciously the social framework that supported its existence. In other words, with Adams's proposed remedy for the labor problem, the middle-class ideal of the entrepreneur remained active and unhampered while monopolists and financiers were to be checked by the State.

In sum, one may say that Henry Carter Adams attempted to discover the causes of labor militancy and anticapitalist senti-ment in order to restore the American system to stability. That stability was threatened by the connection that labor had made between political and economic issues as manifest in its growing interest and sympathy for socialism. The solution to the threat, Adams suspected, was to be found in disconnecting these issues.

For Adams, politics involved only those issues where ques-tions of autonomy were overt and manifest as in the relation between labor, the public, and the monopolies as industries of "increasing returns." On the other hand, questions involving only labor and capital were considered to be questions relevant only to economics. Adams believed that he successfully insu-lated these issues from each other with his concept of the job-right. If only the worker could possess a sense of autonomy, he would tend to confine his interests to the specifically eco-nomic realm; wider political questions would be rendered su-perfluous. Adams was convinced of the validity of his ideas, all that was necessary was to convince others so that they would be implemented. He deplored the fact that

> the leaders of the workingmen in this country have so confused the labor question with the monopoly ques-tion . . . for this confusion leads the conservative public to oppose every change in industrial affairs, thinking all changes to be necessarily in the direction of socialism.[23]

Henry Adams determined the cause of the labor problem and proposed a feasible solution. As far as he was concerned, the State was responsible for safeguarding the viability of the political-economic system by regulating those "industries of increasing returns" which proved to be "irresponsible." Yet, with regard to most economic affairs, the legislative arm of the state was to remain inactive. That is, while collective bargaining was deemed a necessity, it was not to be instituted by legislative enactment but, rather, by means of a new interpretation of the existing law.[24]

In effect, Adams remained confident that the functionaries of the American State would eventually come to recognize their role in the maintenance of the foundations of the system. Given the outline of his proposals, the type of system that was to be maintained was clearly the ideal of the nineteenth-century middle class. It was, perhaps, due to this confidence in the correctness of his ideas and in the leadership of the nation that Adams devoted much less time to the analysis of labor problems after 1900. In any case, Henry Carter Adams's ideas did not generate much support from the leading business interests of the day. The reasons for the absence of an immediate affinity between his ideas and the interests of business are not difficult to determine. In the first place, Adams's theoretical analysis denied the unique nature of the American political-economic system and consistently criticized the unfettered operation of laissez-faire. In addition, he singled out monopolies (industries of "increasing returns") as bearing the greatest responsibility for the generation of the labor problem. Secondly, Adams's proposals for practical reform were inextricably connected to his theoretical analysis. Though Adams's suggestions for reform might be of utility to enlightened businessmen, the fact that those suggestions were embedded within his interpretation of the labor movement made them unpalatable to big business interests. As Adams himself acknowledged, many of the criticisms he directed against American capitalism were quite similar to those advanced by "socialistic writers."[25]

Yet, Adams's departure from the scene did not mark the end of the traditional middle-class concern with the labor movement in America. As will be discussed in the next chapter, the ideas of John Commons emerged to fill the void in an era which would witness the decline of the middle class. In this sense, Commons represented the culmination of the middle-class concern with labor.

7 John Commons and the ___ Pre-Wisconsin Years _____

JOHN R. COMMONS WAS ONE with Richard Ely and Henry Adams in his intent to render the middle-class conception of American capitalism more stable and secure. As he put it in his autobiography, "I was trying to save capitalism by making it good."[1] He shared other similarities with Ely and Adams. The most important of these were his rural, middle-class origin, and his strong religious background which inculcated him with the values of individual initiative and responsibility. Important influences in this regard could be found in his mother whom he described as having adhered to "the strict orthodoxy of Calvinism," and in his father who was characterized as "a follower of Spencer—light of evolutionism and individualism."[2] In fact, so solidly a part of the culture of nineteenth-century middle-class America was Commons that he was shocked to hear Ely denounce Spencer at a meeting of the American Economics Association in 1888. Commons, himself, later attributed this trauma to a background of "Hoosierism, Republicanism, Presbyterianism and Spencerism."[3]

That element which appears to most significantly distinguish Commons from his predecessors is his educational background. In one sense, this made Commons the most traditional of the theorists considered thus far. It may be recalled that both Ely and Adams studied in the United States and Europe and both obtained advanced degrees in economics. None of this was true regarding Commons. His education was strictly American and, what is most noteworthy, limited in the formal sense. In fact, if one considers Commons's academic history he appears very nearly a complete failure.

As an undergraduate Commons attended Oberlin College. Looking back upon those days in the middle 1930s, he offered these thoughts on a "breakdown" he suffered in 1885:

> Coming out from a Greek examination, a fierce blow from outside seemed to hit inside my head. . . . Then I spent three months wandering through the woods about Oberlin, until the end of the school year. . . . When it came to graduation . . . the faculty permitted me to take oral "make-up" examinations, which the dear professors said were poor but none would stand in the way of my graduation.[4]

After graduating from Oberlin, Commons went to Johns Hopkins University to seek an advanced degree. Unfortunately, his formal academic abilities again proved wanting:

> Within a year and a half came my usual fate. I failed completely on a history examination. . . . So I had only two years of graduate work and never reached the degree of Ph.D., the sign manual of a scholar . . . my degrees came as honorary degrees.[5]

Upon acknowledging his shortcomings as a student, Commons attempted to obtain a university instructorship but, at first, was only able to serve as an assistant to Richard Ely at Johns Hopkins. Apparently, Ely had a high regard for Commons and permitted him to work on the first edition of his *Outlines of Economics*, and to teach a course on John Stuart Mill. By 1890 Ely was confident enough to recommend Commons as an instructor to Wesleyan University. However, it appears that Commons was no more successful at teaching than he was at studying, for within nine months he was formally terminated for "failure as a teacher."[6]

Still, Ely saw hope for young Commons and for a time was associated with him in the American Institute of Christian Sociology. Finally, in 1895, Commons was able to obtain another teaching position, this time at Syracuse University. That same year he was fired from the post for what he termed "radicalism." Whether or not this was accurate is difficult to determine. What renders Commons's claim somewhat dubious, however, is that prior to his appointment to Syracuse he declared openly to the chancellor of that University, "[I am] . . . a socialist, a single-taxer, a free silverite, a greenbacker, a municipal-ownerist, a member of the Congregationalist Church."[7] Furthermore, while at Syracuse Commons engaged in rather eccentric behavior for an instructor. As he related one unusual incident:

> To set the criminology class athinking I brought in a half-crazy pauper-tramp, whom I had found somehow, to lecture on his well-remembered but disorderly experiences. . . . He certainly was a success with the class, but for two weeks he kept breaking into the classes of other professors, demanding an opportunity to lecture. I was suppressed by the concerted action of my fellow professors.[8]

In addition, Commons admitted that, in terms of the other university instructors, he was something of an anomaly. This seems the more likely reason for his dismissal than Commons's stated reason for his termination at Syracuse. As Commons stated at another time:

> Henceforth, for more than forty years, they [students and faculty] could see that I was not an authority, did not know much of anything, but was getting ideas from them and incorporating their ideas into mine.[9]

These matters are mentioned, not to denigrate Commons as an academic, but, rather, to bring to light three important facts. First, Commons exhibited a tendency toward inconsistency not only in terms of performance but also in terms of his reportage of events. Second, throughout his early career, Commons was closely associated with Richard Ely. He worked with Ely at the Institute for Christian Sociology, studied under Ely at Johns Hopkins, and later served as his assistant. Clearly, Ely exhibited a strong faith in Commons and assisted him on a number of occasions, despite the latter's continued failures. Finally, Commons admitted that throughout most of his academic career his own work relied heavily upon the ideas of others. In that sense, Commons did not, himself, assert any claim of authority or originality.

For a time the Syracuse termination marked the end of an academic career for Commons. Upon leaving Syracuse he took a job constructing price indices and, when fired from that position, obtained an appointment on the Industrial Commission formed by President McKinley.[10] When he completed his work with the Commission in 1902, Commons ventured to New York and obtained a position with the National Civic Federation, an association of business and labor leaders which attempted to introduce trade agreements between capital and labor onto the industrial scene. Commons secured the position after speaking with Ralph Easley, the secretary for the group.

According to Commons's own reports, he was greatly influenced by Easley and his experiences while employed by the NCF. However, it is somewhat problematic as to whether or not, in fact, it was Easley who was so influential. This is true in that, again, by his own report, Commons indicated that the real dynamo behind the NCF was Marcus Hanna, the Ohio politician and industrialist, to whom Easley was directly subordinate. What moves one to question Commons's attribution of influence are the striking similarities of Hanna's ideas with those later to be espoused by Commons. One may gauge this similarity by a speech Hanna delivered in 1902:

> My experience has taught me, my friends, that the employer because of his position has the most to do, and it must be expected that the employers, at least in the beginning of this educational work, should go more than half way. . . . I believe in organized labor . . . because it is a demonstrated fact that where the concerns and interests of labor are entrusted to able and honest leadership, it is much easier for those who represent the employers to come into close contact with the laborer . . . to accomplish results quicker and better. . . .
> There has been a tendency in this country . . . to what is called socialism. Everything that is America is primarily opposed to socialism . . . [yet] there are extremists who

are teaching the semi-ignorant classes labor theories. . . .
This is a condition which must be met. . . . There is no
question concerning our body politic to-day that should
command deeper or more serious thought. There is nothing in the organization of society in this country that can
afford to permit the growth of socialistic ideas.[11]

The preceding statements are exceedingly important in that
they indicate, in part, the great influence that work with the
NCF was to have on Commons's thought. Commons earlier in
his career labeled himself a socialist, although he came to alter
this. One may recognize such in his remarks against socialist
influence in the AFL circa 1915:

two representatives of the American Federation unions,
Mr. J. B. Lennon, formerly president of the Journeymen
Tailor's national union, and Mr. James O'Connell, formerly president of the Machinists international union, had
been displaced in their organizations by the socialistic element . . . I thought they might see this big issue [the trend
of socialism within the AFL] that was developing. . . . I ar-
ranged a conference for them and myself with Mr. Gompers at his office. . . . I wanted Gompers at last to see . . .
that if it came to an issue, I was standing for his own
ideals of American unionism.[12]

Aside from demonstrating the fact of Commons's change regarding socialism, one is directed toward the conclusion that
his experiences with the NCF had much to do with this transformation in his thought. Corroboration of this may be found
in Commons's own attribution for the source of his distrust of
labor intellectuals. Here, we find Commons attesting to the impact of his NCF activities during the 1902 steel strike: "It was
here that I first learned to distrust the "intellectuals" as leaders
in labor movements. . . . I always look for them and try to clear
them out from all negotiations between capital and labor and
from the councils of labor."[13]

As Commons put it toward the end of his life, "the place of
the economist was that of adviser to the leaders, if they wanted

him, and not that of the propagandist to the masses."[14] In this sense, he seemed to be closer to Adams's conception of the proper role of the political economist as opposed to that of the early Ely.

Commons was, however, consistently inconsistent and, in this regard, clearly differed from Ely and Adams. As shall be seen later, Commons argued that the development of the American labor movement followed a process of "natural selection." While this idea was central to his theory of American labor in 1918, within only a few years he was arguing for a polar point of view. As he was to state in his *Legal Foundations of Capitalism* in 1923:

> Economic theory, since the time of the Physiocrats, has endeavored to get rid of the human will and to explain economic phenomena in terms of physical and hedonistic forces . . . [we see this in] the natural rights and physical equilibrium stage of blind evolution that followed Darwin. . . . But a volitional theory takes exactly the opposite point of view. Economic phenomena . . . are the result of artificial selection and not natural selection.[15]

Such inconsistencies appear natural to Commons in that even a cursory review of his work brings evidence of such ambivalence to the fore. One final example is in order. In his *Institutional Economics* and in his autobiography, *Myself*, both written in 1934, Commons assumed contradictory positions regarding the nature of society. In *Myself* Commons appears to view society as a reality premised upon disharmony and conflict of interest. Yet, in his *Institutional Economics* one reads that, "society is only a word whose meaning is the concerted action of all participants in a going concern."[16] Aside from the turn from realism toward nominalism, one is also presented with a movement from conflict toward harmony.

Such quick transformations have not gone unnoticed by other writers. Joseph Dorfman noted:

> Commons' inconsistencies and shifts were the by-products of a mind groping with the utmost sincerity for ways

and means of achieving the harmonious working together
and progress of the various interest [groups in society] ...
his work evidenced that conflict, often unconscious, so
characteristic of the reformer-intellectual.[17]

While these conflicting qualities characterized Commons's
work throughout his career, we shall be primarily interested in
the manner in which they affected his labor theory. That is,
while Commons's efforts, over time, suffered from inconsistencies, so did, in particular, his consideration of the labor movement. It shall be demonstrated in the next chapter that it was
Commons's attempt to combine the earlier ideas of Ely and
Adams that contributed to the problematic nature of his work.

First, however, it is necessary to indicate the manner in
which Commons came finally to find his niche in academia at
the University of Wisconsin. Immediately, one is struck by the
important role of Commons's former teacher, Richard Ely. As
Commons would later describe it, Ely "worked-up" a position
for him at Wisconsin after consulting Ralph Easley, Commons's
superior in the NCF. The university position became available
to him in 1904. As Commons recorded it, he moved to Wisconsin with the clear intent to write a labor history.

The terms of his appointment prove to be extremely interesting. First, Commons was to be paid the same salary at Wisconsin
as he had received from the NCF. What is more, the university
was to advance but half that sum. The remainder was raised by
Ely, already at Wisconsin, who secured donations from private
capitalists.[18] Thus, it was in this fashion that Commons's work
on labor history and theory was financed. As Commons himself
indicated, during the course of research for his labor volumes,
"I visited my friend from Civic Federation days, V. Everit Macy,
a donor of $10,000 to the expenses of my labor history, and a
friend of Cornelius [Vanderbilt]."[19]

After 1910, when work on the monumental, ten-volume
Documentary History of American Industrial Society was completed, Commons's work in labor history and theory was directly financed from a fund established by Andrew Carnegie.[20] By
1910 Commons completed the first steps in the final construc-
tion of the now famous Wisconsin School of labor theory.

It is clear that Commons was well aware of his benefactors. That is, his financial and emotional attachments to the turn-of-the-century captains of industry, those idealized entrepreneurs, were publicly observed and proclaimed. Said Commons regarding his patrons, "I always found in myself a bushwacking admiration for great warriors, great desperadoes, great captains of industry, who could hold up a stage coach or a nation or the whole capitalist system." Observing Andrew Carnegie during an appearance before the Industrial Commission in 1914, Commons stated, "I just sat there and enjoyed Carnegie—a laughing Robin Hood of the capitalist system."[21] As did the earlier theorists, Commons admired the middle-class ideal of the ambitious and shrewd business entrepreneur.

8 John Commons and the Wisconsin — School in Full Bloom

WHEN JOHN COMMONS COMPLETED the multivolume *Documentary History of Industrial Society* in 1910, the decisive experiences gained through his employment with the NCF were already behind him. In these volumes one may perceive the raw material from which Commons later fashioned his labor theory. Perhaps the most important aspect of that huge effort was Commons's "discovery" that the earliest, continuous organization of wage-earners in the United States was that of the Philadelphia Shoemakers. These workers did, in 1792, associate with the primary intent of maintaining and advancing their wages.[1]

What made this historical fact so significant was that it served as a refutation of what Commons took to be Marx's theory of capitalist development. That is, Commons arrived at the certainty that the development of the workers' struggle in America was necessarily and significantly different from that encountered upon the European continent. One may appreciate the import of this single fact for Commons if it is realized that the following appraisal appeared in the first volume of his *History of Labour in the United States*:

> Our chronology also runs counter to the theory that the origin of class struggles is to be traced to the technical evolution of industry and the ownership of the "tools of production." Labour organization and the "class struggle" of wage-earners in America preceded by many years the factory system which finally separated the worker from ownership of the tools.[2]

It would appear that Commons was arguing for a thesis to assert that America was somehow unique; the development of a labor movement in America could not, therefore, be expected to parallel the development of those in other nations. As Commons proclaimed in the introduction to his labor history, "Labour movements in America have arisen from peculiar American conditions; and it is by understanding these conditions that we shall be able to distinguish movements and methods of organization from those of other countries."[3] What Commons intended to indicate was that American conditions, as witnessed by the case of the early shoemakers, propelled the labor movement toward a peculiar program and manner of organization. Specifically, this program—as Commons saw it—was a strictly economistic brand of unionism, or "job consciousness." The organization that officially embodied this concept in 1910 was the AFL. Just as the goals of the shoemakers might be considered as the pure expression of the desires of American wage-earners, so the AFL might be considered as a latter-day realization of those very same desires.

As Selig Perlman, Commons's closest protégé, was to indicate at a later date, the AFL was the most prominent working-men's organization because it was the most "fit," because, "of its discovery of a program of job solidarism least repugnant to deeply rooted American individualism."[4] Volume 1 of Commons's labor history stated that "by a kind of *Natural Selection* [my emphasis] a more pragmatic or "opportunistic" philosophy . . . has taken form in the American Federation of Labor."[5]

In one sense, then, the Wisconsin theory in its most developed form would maintain that a rather narrow and economistic unionism was, from the beginning, natural to America. This argument, however, faced certain difficulties. What, for example, might be said regarding the great labor upheavals of the past, or the growing union militancy with which Henry Adams had been so concerned? It was with regard to this question that Commons's most original contribution to the analysis of labor in America was to be found.

Commons, unlike Adams, did not view labor militancy and the growth of socialist sympathies among workingmen as inherent or permanent in the capitalist social organization of America. Rather, as previously indicated, he considered the American movement as unique or exceptional in that economism or job consciousness was the natural expression of labor in the United States.

Enumerating the factors responsible for this, Commons contended that American labor would never assume a radical orientation due to the early establishment of universal manhood suffrage, the rapid extension of market areas, the court system, and the political organization of American parties. Most important+ly, "the condition which seems to distinguish most clearly the history of labour in America from its history in other countries . . . [is] the wide expanse of free land."[6] This factor was said to leave open to American workers the chance to employ their own initiative to "get ahead" and, perhaps, remove themselves from the ranks of wage-earners. The net effect of this was supposed to be the retention of the belief in mobility and the value of individual initiative. Of course, these were prime values to the middle-class American, and Commons seemed to recapitulate them in his ideas of the nature of the American political-economic system.

How might these assumptions deal with the irrefutable facts with which Henry Adams had been so concerned? Commons did not deny the growth of labor militancy or socialistic sympathies within the American movement. He simply did not view them as natural or inherent to capitalist America or to the labor movement in the United States. In this regard, Commons was no vulgar apologist for the status quo as he is sometimes portrayed by the contemporary Left.[7]

Basically, socialism might be a natural, antithetical expression to capitalism elsewhere, but not in America, according to Commons. It was not that radical tendencies were absent, but simply that they were not natural. In this regard, Commons appeared to retain the faith that Ely expressed in the labor movement in his early works. Yet, by virtue of his recognition of the seriousness of the socialist challenge, Commons was not content to leave the matter to the eventual triumph of that faith alone. Commons, as did Adams, appreciated the necessity of finding an immediate and practical solution to the crisis facing the nation. The central theoretical question Commons had to address, then, was this—What caused so unnatural a development as the growth of socialism within the labor movement of the United States? This question served as the basis for John Commons's theoretical efforts. The very posing of this question was significant in that it reversed the question which was earlier posed by Henry Adams, namely, How might the wholly expected advance of socialism in the United States be forestalled?

How did this reversal come about? For an indication one must consider developments in the larger society. First, however, it is necessary to indicate the theory by which Commons explained the "unnatural" occurrences within American labor. That is, one must discern Commons's explication of labor activity between the eras of the Philadelphia Shoemakers and the AFL.

As Commons indicated on a number of occasions, "the money question" and the business cycle were the most important of all labor problems. According to him, "the business cycle first demoralizes labor, then pauperizes labor, then coerces labor. The most important labor problem was the stabilization of employers' wholesale prices."[8]

Commons clearly tied the history of American labor to the history of the business cycle. This, in fact, was true of all labor movements. However, for Commons the important factor was the severe fluctuations to be found in the American business cycle. Due to these "excessive" fluctuations, the American labor movement was moved further away from its "natural" course. Commons noted that, "the repeating cycle of politics and trade unionism, political struggle and economic struggle, political organisation and economic organisation, marks out the course of this history of [American] labour." Further:

> While the area of market competition has extended more widely than in other countries the level of prices and wages across this area has arisen and fallen more excessively. . . . In periods of rising prices, when the cost of living was outleaping the rise of wages, when business was prosperous and labour in demand, then aggressive strikes, trade unionism, class struggle, suddenly spread over the industrial sec-

tions of the country. At the other extreme, in the periods of falling prices, with their depression of business and distress by unemployment, labour, in its helplessness and failure of defensive strikes, has turned to politics, panaceas, or schemes of universal reform.[9]

Thus, Commons sought to explain the aberrations of American labor through the unusually wide fluctuations to the business cycle. Yet, by the early 1900s he became convinced that this heretofore all-important factor—the business cycle—was no longer operative in a significant way. This was true at least in terms of its affect upon labor organization. Commons was to write in 1918 that as the 1880s drew to a close,

the labour movement had attained such a degree of class organization that, compared with former years, a transition from prosperity to depression no longer led to appreciable change in its character. . . . Industrial development ceased to be completely overshadowed by periodic fluctuations in markets.[10]

While this indicated that the American proletariat had fully emerged as a class, it said nothing regarding the programs of that class. Commons, however, believed that he successfully isolated an important causative element regarding such. This was to be found in what he termed the "industrial and economic stages of capitalism." Commons explained these terms:

The historical stages which determine survival may be distinguished as Industrial and Economic. They are inseparable . . . the industrial stages are the changes in technology named by Marx. . . . The economic stages are the changes in institutions which we designate as the stages of Scarcity, Abundance, and Stabilization. . . .

Capitalism is not a single or static concept. It is an evolutionary concept of three historic stages[which correlate with scarcity, abundance and stabilization], Merchant Capitalism, Employer Capitalism, Banker Capitalism. The last

named is dominant, owing to the prevalence of the credit
system, while the first arose out of the extension of markets and the second out of technology.[11]

Commons appeared to imply that until the arrival of banker
capitalism, the industrial and economic stages were in a condition of disequilibrium. In other words, they were not coordi-
nated and this gave rise to instability. This was a major contributor to the wide fluctuations of the business cycle.

Commons carried this analysis further by correlating his
stages of capitalism with the development of workingmen's phi-
losophies. In essence, he maintained that a philosophy of anarchism arose from merchant capitalism, communism from employer capitalism, and a philosophy of "live and let live" from
banker capitalism.[12] What is significant here is that this scheme
intimated a reconciliation with Henry Adams's earlier analysis
of the American situation. That is, based upon the idea that employer capitalism had given rise to a philosophy of communism,
Commons did not have to refute Adams's ideas. This was true in
that Commons's theory periodicized or relativized that of Adams and thereby indicated that, while not in error, it was irrelevant to the contemporary American society characterized, as it
was, by banker capitalism.

In actuality, Commons's theory did much more than simply
relativize that which had been proposed by Adams. In effect,
the question Commons posed for theory opened up a whole
new manner of approaching the problem of labor in America.
Where Adams viewed the increased militancy of workers as inherent to capitalist social organization itself, Commons was arguing that it was merely a passing moment. Commons seemed
to be struggling toward the idea that labor troubles were a consequence of anomie, which inevitably accompanied social evolution in the direction of a fully developed capitalist society.

Labor problems and socialist sympathies among the American proletariat were not built into the capitalist organization
of society but, rather, were the expressions of the incomplete
development of that society. As Durkheim earlier argued that
the division of labor was, in itself, no cause for social break-

down, so Commons appeared to be asserting that capitalism in America, in itself, was no cause for the enthronement of socialism upon the labor movement of the United States. What is more, Commons's ideas on the business cycle and the stages of capitalist development appeared to provide a more concrete basis for the early Ely's ultimate faith in the virtues of the labor movement. As may be recalled, Commons was a participant with Ely in the American Institute for Christian Sociology, and fully countenanced Ely's moralistic views. In effect, then, Commons attempted to resurrect the originally sanguine outlook of Ely.

It is significant, therefore, that Commons was contending that it was practically impossible for socialism to become the rallying cry for the workers of America. He felt that once the disturbing elements were removed from the social scene by industrial and economic evolution, the American workers could realize their natural propensities which were dictated by their environment. That is, the economistic or job conscious unionism, which Commons viewed as natural to America, could realize itself, objectively, once all extraneous and interfering factors were removed by the march of history.

With this Commons not only relativized and rendered somewhat irrelevant Adams's ideas but, apparently, seemed to banish the subjective element from the workings of history. Adams's theory posited that the middle-class ideal of capitalism in America could be saved if businessmen only acted in a more responsible fashion; that is, if they ceased to act only in accord with their immediate interests which tended to undermine the very foundation of the capitalist economy. As such, the Adams theory recognized the element of contingency in history—the advance of socialism might be stopped if capital modified its activity.

Commons's theory, on the other hand, transformed this contingency into necessity. That is, capitalism in America would be saved, not because of the enlightened actions of a class but, instead, because unique American conditions and circumstances ordained that this would occur. This view clearly removed the responsibility for the development of capitalism from human agents and posited it with the impersonal workings of history.

Where Adams called for a new interpretation of the existing law on the part of the courts, believing as he did that the members of the capitalist class would not rise above their immediate, individual interests, Commons maintained that such a proposal was moot. For him it was unnecessary to quarrel over the thrust of truly responsible action or the place of the courts in guaranteeing such. The only time that governmental action might be necessary was in the case of monopolies or trusts.[13] For the most part, however, Commons contended that the arrival of banker capitalism would render it immediately clear to both labor and capital that some sort of "live and let live" policy was necessary and inevitable. That is, the contemporary constitution of society would dictate to all concerned that both capitalist and worker organizations should be viewed as permanent parts of society which could not be removed without threatening the entire social fabric.

Expressing no diffidence with regard to these ideas, Commons counseled all, especially the government, to remain at a distance from the affairs of capital and labor. That is, so certain was he of the correctness of his ideas that he would accept only the voluntary trade agreement as an accurate expression of capital and labor "stabilization" under banker capitalism:

> The basic idea of the trade agreement is that of collective bargaining rather than arbitration. . . . The agreement is made by direct negotiation between the two organised groups [of capital and labor], and the sanction which each holds over the head of the other is the strike or lockout.[14]

In short, Commons's theory differed from that of Adams, but seemed to be similar to that of Ely, in that it viewed militancy as essentially a result of the incompleteness of capitalist development. Commons expanded this idea in his belief that once markets were fully extended and industrial technology developed, the way was clear for the emergence of banker capitalism. Once this arose, society would become stabilized since all sides would somehow recognize the value of accepting the existence of the other.

While this mutual acceptance (as found in the trade agreement) was voluntary on the immediate level it was in fact, a necessary consequence of a new stage of social organization. In this sense, what appeared to be a voluntary agreement of individuals and groups was actually determined by the dictates of historical evolution. With Commons it was no longer a question of coercing capital or labor to behave more responsibly, for such would occur naturally with the emergence of banker capitalism. It was in this manner that John Commons explained the realization of American labor's supposed natural propensity for economistic unionism.

Commons's experiences with the NCF no doubt provided support for his theoretical views. In fact, such experiences may have served as an essential underpinning for his ideas. This is true in that, steeped in the individualism of nineteenth-century middle-class America, with no direct exposure to the new social thoughts from abroad, socialist collectivism and the concept of proletarian revolution could only appear as terrible, unnatural aberrations of what was right and proper—as something utterly foreign which no true American could embrace.

It was during his service with the NCF that Commons witnessed some American unionists coming to terms with capitalists in voluntary agreements and thereby behaving in a manner contrary to socialist hopes. Also during his tenure with the NCF Commons became convinced that true American unionism was premised upon voluntarism and job-consciousness—characteristics which were more compatible with his own values. Thus, when Commons's NCF experiences are viewed within the context of his labor theory, they reflect the manner in which he sustained support for his own values and beliefs.

It may be recalled that Commons was employed by the NCF from 1902 to 1904. It was precisely at that time that the American labor movement was making a major advance. Between the years 1897 and 1904 the AFL saw its membership leap from 264,825 to 1,676,200. What is more, total union membership jumped nearly five times as the number of wage-earners organized into unions moved from 447,000 to well over two million.[15]

Clearly, an observer with these union increases in mind might infer that American unionism represented a successful undertaking. Furthermore, this period included the most strenuous efforts of the NCF to reconcile capital and labor through the institution of trade agreements. Specifically, the NCF exercised its greatest influence between the years 1900 and 1905.[16] And, it was precisely the trade agreement that Commons was wont to use as an indicant of union success.[17] Selig Perlman points out that during the early 1900s "another proof of trade union progress is found in the spread of trade agreements." He continues, "The idea of a joint partnership of organized labor and organized capital in the management of industry, which, ever since the fifties, had been struggling for acceptance, finally showed signs of coming to be materialized."[18]

Thus, it is not incomprehensible that Commons should take these experiences to serve as the basis of his theory of the labor movement. That is, the experience with the NCF, which he held to be so important to himself, served to bolster and provide credence to his ideas concerning American labor. These early experiences appeared to lend validity to the values and ideals of one raised within the bosom of middle-class America.

This experience could only serve to reinforce the beliefs and values of someone like Commons—who was already predisposed to view anything that jeopardized individualism and personal initiative negatively. However, the belief that American labor was by nature conciliatory and economistic was soon to be rendered most problematic by historical events. Due to the impact of recession, beginning in 1903 and lasting until 1908, employers engaged in what labor historians have characterized as "the employers' mass offensive." Basically, this represented an open-shop campaign which intended to repel the advances won by workers since 1897.[19] So successful was this "offensive" that trade union membership declined from 2,072,700 in 1904 to nearly 1,900,000 in 1906.[20] In fact, during the years 1904 through 1910 there was practically no increase in union membership. Membership levels did not exceed the level of 1904 until 1911.[21]

With this in mind it is understandable that, by 1905, the idea of the trade agreement lost the enthusiasm it once enjoyed. It was at that date—Commons had already severed his connection with the NCF to go to Wisconsin—that the NCF shifted its activities and propagandized against the evils of socialism rather than for the concept of the trade agreement.[22] Thus, Commons was long gone from NCF employment by the time his ideas were dashed against hard reality. As will be seen, Commons continued to judge this reality on the basis of his earlier subjective experiences. It was precisely these experiences that supported his abiding beliefs and values.

As Thomas Brooks indicated, due to the problems associated with AFL boycott policies and the growth of employer opposition to unionism, around 1912 there was a general drift toward radicalism within American labor.[23] Coincident with this was a great leap in union membership. Between 1910 and 1913 the total membership increased by over a third.[24] This advance, however, was not uniformly distributed throughout the labor movement. If one considers those industries experiencing the greatest increases, it is found that they were the clothing (68 percent membership leap) and mining (60 percent increase) industries.[25] What is more, by 1912, socialists were in full control of the miners' and the machinists' unions; the International Ladies Garment Workers Union, which possessed a distinct left-wing ideology, was primarily responsible for the growth of unionism in the clothing industry.[26] In essence, then, labor was moving forward after 1910 and the greatest progress was to be found among those organizations with a socialistic orientation.

Not only was 1910 through 1915 a period of increasing radicalism within labor, but it was also a time of escalating violence in the never-ending dispute over autonomy between capital and labor. So much so that Graham Adams characterized the period by saying, "A common unifying theme emerged from the [governmental] inquiries [into industrial violence] . . . . Almost every strike, irrespective of origin, appeared to have erupted into violence which threatened the structure of society."[27]

It is here, during a period of increasing violence and socialist sympathy within the ranks of American workers, that one encounters John Commons steadfastly embracing the ideas consistent with his background and early administrative experiences. While serving on the United States Commission on Industrial Relations, Commons stated omnisciently that the men of labor "were being misled by the general unrest into throwing their movement into politics."[28]

When the Industrial Commission completed its research in 1915, Commons refused to sign the final report which identified the causes of unrest as follows: workers did not receive a fair share of wealth, workers suffered too often from unemployment, most workers are convinced that they are denied justice and, finally, workers resent the denial of their right to organize into unions.[29] Commons, however, came to recognize the import of Henry Adams's considerations of labor. As did Adams, Commons came to attribute a fundamental cause for the exacerbation of social conflicts to "confusion" on the part of working-class leaders.[30] Neither Commons nor Adams appeared to consider that what they perceived as confusion might have been the recognition by working people of their own, distinct interest in society.

Despite Commons's objections and warnings, the trend of events as described above continued during World War I. Though the organized workers were provided with organizing and bargaining rights through the influence of the War Labor Conference Board, labor protests continued to mount.[31] As Gary Fink related, the rank and file, as opposed to the national leaders within the AFL, consistently rejected the conservative philosophy of voluntarism.[32] Shortly after the cessation of the war, the *Nation* reported:

> The most extraordinary phenomenon of the present time, the most incalculable in its after effects, the most menacing in its threat of immediate consequences, and the most alluring in its possibilities of ultimate good, is the unprecedented revolt of the rank and file.[33]

Though real wages were, in fact, rising during the war years, labor protest continued to mount. In fact, the years 1916 to 1918 witnessed an average of 2.4 times as many workers out on strike as compared to 1915.[34] Should one recall the earlier consideration of the autonomy issue, the causes of labor militancy are not difficult to perceive.

Not only did the war serve as a stimulus to business but, furthermore, it accelerated the pace of technological innovation.[35] In addition, the government's wartime interest in maintaining the quality and advancing the overall amount of production provided an impetus for increased standardization and the widescale use of the techniques of scientific management.[36] In effect, then, the renewed radicalism and militancy was coeval with renewed threats against autonomy in the workplace.

The above connection is especially cogent when one realizes that rank and file revolt immediately after the war spread, in the form of wildcat strikes, to even such conservative centers of unionism as the printing trades.[37] The most important of such strikes, however, was to be found within the railroad industry. The railroad industry was where standardization and more efficient production techniques were most assiduously fostered by the government. As one economic historian recorded this situation:

> [certain] . . . phases of Government control have had more enduring result. One of these was the extension of standardization, which was . . . applied with unprecedented concentration of purpose during the crisis of WWI. . . . For example, the principle of standardization was extended appreciably in the production of locomotives and railway rolling stock. This activity of the Government merged insensibly into another, which also had an abiding effect—the campaign to lessen waste in industry.[38]

The question immediately presents itself, was John Commons such an unabashed apologist as to discount reality through the promulgation of his own theory? That is, since banker capitalism had not brought about the stability he had expected, how was it possible to insist that his theory of the labor movement was valid? In addition there is a more subtle question that cannot be ignored. Why should Commons insist that he had to save capitalism when his theory indicated that salvation required no subjective intervention since it was automatic or inherent to the social evolution of capitalist America?

To some writers on the Left, it would seem as if the first

question was answered in the affirmative. For example, Philip Foner, in the preface to the first volume of his *History of the Labor Movement in the United States*, commented that "the volumes of the *History of Labor in the United States* became in effect an apologia of Gompersism—craft unionism, no politics in the unions, and community of interest between labor and capital."[39]

Such a characterization of Commons does not, however, appear to be accurate. Commons did not so much discount reality as attempt to explain it with the middle-class world view. Even then, his explanation did not constitute an ex post facto attempt to distort history to bring it into conformity with his theory. Rather, it was the effect of the lens that he employed to examine social reality; and that lens was provided to him through his background and social situation, and bolstered by his earlier experiences. In fact the use of this specific lens—the manner in which he did analyze reality—constituted his original contribution to labor theory.

As indicated earlier, growing up in nineteenth-century middle-class America, Commons took individualism in terms of responsibility and initiative as the touchstone of what was true and moral. Due to this upbringing, which was infused with Spencerism and Calvinism, he viewed socialism as distinctly alien to what he had been taught was inbred in all Americans. Thus, socialism and un-Americanism tended to become synonymous in his mind. One finds Commons giving expression to such thoughts in 1907, a few years after his departure from the NCF:

> We are trying to look beneath the surface and to inquire whether there are not factors of heredity and race more fundamental than those of education and environment. We find that our democratic theories and forms of government were fashioned by but one of many races and peoples which have come within their practical operation, and that that race, the so-called Anglo-Saxon, developed them out of its own insular experience unhampered by inroads of alien stock.[40]

Thus, Commons did tend to think in terms of an American versus un-American dichotomy. What is more, he posited this as the central problem facing the nation, and in fact equated this un-Americanism with radicalism; saying, "If in America our boasted freedom from the evils of social classes fails to be vindicated in the future, the reasons will be found in the immigration of races and classes incompetent to share in our democratic opportunities."[41]

To control this danger, however, it was not necessary to refuse admittance to all immigrants to the nation, as some were demanding at the time. Instead, some could come to enjoy life in America for the following reason:

> It is not physical amalgamation that unites mankind; it is mental community. To be great a nation need not be one of blood, it must be one of mind. Racial inequality and inferiority are fundamental only to the extent that they prevent mental and moral assimilation.[42]

What is required to safeguard Americanism, then, is simply a conscious polity of assimilation which would inculcate the correct ideals into immigrant minds. It seemed as if Commons believed that socialism could be removed by a process of enculturation. Indeed, this seems to be the case when one considers Commons's following comments:

> The American unions, in fact, grow out of American conditions, and are an American product . . . Labor organization is essentially the outcome of American freedom, both as a corrective to the evils of free competition and as an exercise of the privilege of free association. . . .
> There is but one thing that stands in the way of complete unionization in many industries; namely a flood of immigration too great for assimilation.[43]

Should we keep these thoughts in mind, later statements by Commons assume a special significance. One may recognize this in an idea he expressed in 1915:

> The recognition of unions through collective bargaining
> would protect business and the nation against politics,
> radicalism, and communism by placing a conservative la-
> bor movement in the strategic position.[44]

Employer recognition of unions through their engagement
in collective bargaining and the institution of trade agreements
with unions would combat socialism and radicalism, but not because these would stall any tendencies inherent to a capitalist
America. Rather, they would institutionalize the supposedly
naturally conservative American movement which would
thereby serve as an ideal and official model to which immigrants might assimilate.[45] It was in this fashion that an element
of subjectivity (i.e., planned action initiated by a specific social
group) was introduced into a theory which earlier appeared as
wholly objective and deterministic.

By this turn, Commons was able to arrive at a position strik-
ingly similar to that earlier proposed by Henry Adams. Commons agreed, in effect, that collective bargaining was a
necessary device to combat socialism. Significantly, however,
Commons did not agree with Adams's reasoning. Whereas
Adams indicated that a trend toward socialism was inherent in
capitalism, Commons denied it. Where Adams indicated that
American workers would become increasingly militant as long
as capitalism was permitted to evolve without subjective intervention and guidance by the state, Commons indicated that
this would be obviated through social evolution.

The most basic difference between Adams and Commons
was that the former was able to discern destabilizing processes
within the American political-economic system itself, while
the latter bifurcated his analysis in terms of intrasystemic as
opposed to extrasystemic influences. To Commons, the growth
of socialism within the labor movement was due to the extrasystemic forces.

It was in this fashion that John Commons was able to maintain his belief in Ely's early and optimistic consideration of
the labor movement in America while simultaneously calling
for the institution of the practical proposals advocated by Hen-

ry Adams. Of the three theorists, Commons's ideas were clearly the ones most bound by the traditional world-view of the nineteenth-century American middle class. Thus, while Commons did come to advocate the reforms originally promulgated by Henry Adams, he was never able to countenance their implementation in the manner indicated in Adams's analysis. That is, with Commons collective bargaining was to come about through the free and voluntary agreement of labor and capital; in no way was the state to be involved.[46]

In this sense, socialism was not the basic threat for Commons. It was secondary, a derivative. In effect, it would not have to be of concern were it not for the influx of immigrants who carted it to America with the rest of their cultural baggage. For Commons, the immigrant had to be separated from his radical ideas and imbued with American institutions and values. One manner in which this might be accomplished was to consciously display American unionism as a model to be emulated by all newcomers. It was for this reason that Commons called for the institutionalization of trade unions by way of collective bargaining. While Adams and Commons, then, arrived at similar proposals which aimed at combating socialism, the routes by which they completed that journey were appreciably different.

Thus, though he did so while operating with different assumptions, John Commons endorsed the tenet of Henry Adams that the old English conception of property had to be superseded by the new concept of the "job-right" as was implicit within the framework of collective bargaining.[47] When ideas of this sort *w* were criticized by the old guard at the time of the completion of Henry Adams's tenure as president of the American Economics Association, Commons was quick to leap to Adams's defense. Said Commons in 1899:

> The function of the political economist is to show that the standpoint of a class is the best standpoint; and he does this even when he claims to speak from the standpoint of society as a whole. . . . Economists have not lost influence as a whole—only those who stand for a class which has passed the day of its political power.[48]

As time went on, Commons was to forget these words and the fact that they were applicable to himself as well as to others. Given his world view and his ability to select appropriate ideas from the earlier work of Ely and Adams, Commons could propagate the idea that American labor found socialism naturally repugnant while simultaneously asserting that the initiation of collective bargaining was necessary to thwart socialist progress in the United States. By intertwining the practical proposals of Adams with fundamental assumptions similar to those which were held by Ely, Commons could do this without appearing totally inconsistent or contradictory. There *is* little reason to doubt that Commons sincerely believed in the validity of this synthetic theory.

Yet, insofar as the premises of John Commons's theory were entirely different from those of Adams's, the policy implications of that theory were open to a variety of interpretations. Such was not the case with Adams's analysis. For Adams, socialism was a natural development of the socio-economic structure of the nation, and therefore, the reform of that structure was essential to combat socialism and labor militancy.

With Commons's theory, the premises did not lead toward a singular, apodictic conclusion. For example, if American workers were, by nature, simply job-conscious it would not be absolutely necessary to institute bargaining on their account. This might be viewed as fortunate from the point of view of the great industrial enterprises in that concessions to labor, no matter how insignificant, might be obviated. What is more, since one intent behind the institutionalization of bargaining in Commons's theory was to dissuade immigrants from persisting in their supposedly radical ways, could not an alternative means be found to achieve that same end? Given the premises of Commons's theory, what would be wrong with providing for assimilation through the use of negative example—suppressing all worker organizations and demands that contradicted the job-consciousness which was assumed to be natural to American workers?

Though Commons, himself, never expressed this latter interpretation, the logic of his theory could not forestall the derivation of such a conclusion. This was especially the case if one aspect of all new political economic theory—the attempt to preserve the traditional middle class notion of democracy—was disregarded.[49] It was the entrepreneurs of the emerging great industrial enterprises who had been a primary source of funding for Commons's theoretical efforts. It did not appear that these patrons were much interested in a traditional middle-class interpretation of democratic theory.[50]

In light of the historical record, it seems clear that the repressive interpretation of Commons's theory was more to the liking of at least some of the new economic elite in the United States. After the First World War an open-shop drive, dubbed "the American Plan," spread across the industrial landscape. Most unions were labeled as radical and subversive organizations, the results of the efforts of foreign influence and agitation.[51] In the eyes of the large-scale, integrated capitalist enterprises, such aggressive action would make it clear to all working people, foreign and native alike, that the American system would brook no organized challenges.[52]

In effect, the repression visited upon the labor movement in the 1920s did have a theoretical basis, namely, the theory of labor in America provided for by Commons's Wisconsin School did have an affinity with the immediate interests of big businessmen.[53] Due to the premises upon which it was founded, the theory of John Commons was open to a variety of interpretations. The interpretation which carried the greatest social weight was the one that proved most suitable to the immediate interests of the new capitalist elite, not those of the traditional middle class.

In reality it was not surprising that the leaders of America's large corporations chose to interpret Commons's ideas in a repressive fashion. A variety of means had been tried to dampen the growing militancy of labor, but the issue of autonomy consistently was thrust into the arena of contention. As was noted in a 1915 journal article:

> [Although] the A.F.L. disclaims any socialistic aspirations, its demands are sufficiently radical. The free right to use

the strike, picket, and boycott to enforce collective bargaining, backed by a powerful organization. . . . Employers were justified, from their point of view, in becoming alarmed.[54]

Various "welfare programs" for workers had been tried at both U.S. Steel and Standard Oil, two of the largest corporations, since the early part of the century. Yet, as John Garrity noted, welfare paternalism failed to develop loyal workers.[55] Within the steel corporation the drive to improve the workers' welfare included the initiation of safety movements, industrial accident prevention programs, and community health work.[56] Perhaps the most famous aspect of the welfare drive was the institution of a stock-ownership plan for employees in 1902. It is interesting to note that the inspiration and leadership for these welfare measures came from the banker's faction within the leadership of the steel corporation. That faction, led by J. P. Morgan and his lieutenants Elbert Gary and George Perkins, was interested in long-run planning and stability for the industry.[57] Welfare programs represented one of the means for the achievement of the above ends.

The Standard Oil Corporation also was busy at improving the welfare of its workers. As early as 1903 the Standard had initiated a non-contributory old-age pension plan for its employees. By 1914 the corporation was reducing the work week of its process employees from eighty-four to seventy-six hours. In addition, the company freely went beyond the requirements of compensation laws and extended comparatively high benefits to workers injured on the job.[58] Gradually, worker welfare programs were instituted in a number of industries and businessmen's associations became interested. For example, by 1911 the program of the National Electric Light Association included accident relief, sickness insurance, service annuities, and savings and profit-sharing plans.[59]

Testifying before the Federal Commission on Industrial Relations in 1915, Ida Tarbell, the noted muckraker, bore witness to a "silent revolution" in industry which had as its goal the application of "the Golden Rule" to relations between capital and labor.[60] Upon his turn to testify before the commission, John D. Rockefeller, Jr. commented that if "fair wages and reasonable living conditions cannot otherwise be provided, dividends must be deferred, or the industry abandoned . . . a corporation should be deemed to consist of its stockholders, directors, officers, and employees . . . the real interests of all are one."[61]

With the above in mind it is understandable how someone such as Commons might be sanguine about the arrival of banker capitalism. It was, after all, the banker's group within the steel corporation that had pressed for improvements in worker welfare and sought the application of the golden rule in employer-employee relations. At the Standard Oil Corporation it was A. C. Bedford, president of Standard of New Jersey by 1916, who called for the introduction of similar measures at his plants. In fact, Elbert Gary of U.S. Steel and A. C. Bedford of the Standard shared certain characteristics:

> The career of Elbert Gary in the United States Steel Corporation presents a significant analogy to that of Bedford in the Jersey company. Gary, too, assumed a newly created board chairmanship and devoted his energies to building good will for his company and stability for the industry.[62]

However, for U.S. Steel and Standard Oil "good will" was not to be obtained from the extension of collective bargaining rights or the recognition of labor unions. The large corporations insisted upon unilateral control over conditions of work at the point of production. This was something that John Commons and his theory never appreciated fully. For the big companies the issue of autonomy remained paramount.

In 1912, not long after the last remnants of union organization were removed from the steel corporation, Raynall Bolling, assistant general-solicitor for U.S. Steel wrote: "The United States Steel Corporation has made no was on unionism. It has acted wholly on the defensive and in defense of the principle of the 'open shop', where employment is not a question of unionism or non-unionism, but of a man's ability and desire to work."[63]

A few months prior to the great steel strike of 1919, Charles Schwab of Bethlehem Steel announced:

> I am not opposed to organized labor. I believe that labor should organize in individual plants or amongst themselves for the better negotiation of labor and the protection of their own rights; but the organization and control of labor in individual plants and manufactures, to my mind, must be representative of the people in those plants. . . . [One of the teachings of the war has been] true democracy. The thing we have to do is to teach, not patronize, to educate. . . . We have to devise ways and means by which capital and labor, that have so often been termed synonymous, shall share equally, not in theory, but in practice. We have got to devise ways and means of education.[64]

The historical record would seem to suggest that the steel corporation believed labor could obtain its finest education through the school of hard knocks. The attempt to bring unionism into steel was beaten back in a particularly bloody fasion in 1919. Strikes and strike leaders were branded as foreign agents, professional agitators, Bolsheviks, and lost souls (i.e., immigrants) unfamiliar with or disloyal to the principles of American government.[65] The lesson the corporation hoped would be drawn from the strike was that unions were but "relics of a preceding age." Elbert Gary formed the following conclusions from the perspective of big steel: "there is at present, in the opinion of the large majority of both employers and employees, no necessity for labor unions; and that no benefit or advantage through them will accrue to anyone except the union leaders."[66]

Thus, by 1920, unions could not hope to exist in the steel industry. This situation was to remain until the New Deal. It is sometimes suggested that the virulent and violent open-shop policies of the big corporations were due to the post-World War I hysteria against radicalism.[67] Certainly, the postwar hysteria played some role in this. However, the stage already had been set for rabid and violent antiunionism on the part of the large corporations prior to America's entrance into the war. This is clear from a consideration of the relationship between capital and labor in big oil. Much has been written on 1919 and steel, but little has been done on the oil industry.

Yet, even before 1917 Standard Oil had paraded charges of anti-Americanism, foreign subversion and radicalism against strikers before the public. This occurred during the 1915 and 1916 strikes at the Bayonne, New Jersey, plant of Standard. Hysterical reactions to labor's challenge to corporate autonomy at the work site did not have to await the postwar "red scare." Some social analysts had recognized the situation and the importance of the autonomy issue already in 1914:

> Business is impatient to see the open shop established. This desire does not seem to be stimulated by an aversion to paying union wages, but rather by a wish to have industrial conditions placid and "controllable." This dislike of dividing power with any force, least of all a union, coupled with the mounting profits and surpluses since 1900, has caused capital to be both temperamentally ready for trouble, and prepared financially to meet it.[68]

There can be no doubt that the profits of the Bayonne plant of Standard Oil of New Jersey were impressive, especially after the war. In 1914 the company's earnings in Bayonne amounted to $332,000. But a year later earnings jumped to over six million dollars.[69] Labor difficulties had not occurred at the Bayonne facility since 1903, at which time a strike occurred for union recognition after a union man was fired by a foreman and replaced by a nonunion worker. The union lost the struggle and shortly thereafter, in line with the scenario of events that had occurred in steel, welfare policies for workers were instituted by the company.[70]

Perhaps because of the lack of labor turmoil after the early part of the century, Bayonne was an attractive site for corporate investment. Between 1909 and 1914 thirty million dollars in new capital was invested in the city, thereby increasing the total by almost 50 percent.[71] One reason for the docility of labor was the large numbers of newly arrived immigrant workers. At the time of the 1915 strike it was estimated that

30 percent of the employees could not read, write, or speak English.

The composition of the work force, heavily Polish and Italian, was not determined by accident:

> In the New Jersy refineries nationality, rather than experience, often was the prime qualification for a job . . . newly arrived immigrants being preferred because they were docile and not inclined to strike. Slavs were regarded as particularly tractable and efficient in the performance of unskilled tasks. . . . Most of the foremen (predominantly Irish) preferred to mix nationalities in their working gangs in order to prevent clannishness.[72]

The 1915 strike began on July 15 after a rumor that wages were to be reduced spread among the men. The average income at the Bayonne plant amounted to but $818 a year.[73] In addition, employees complained bitterly against the treatment they received from the foremen and about the conditions of labor in the plant. The still-cleaners, in particular, were outspoken in their grievances, and were in the vanguard of the strikers' ranks. As *Survey* reported:

> The chief grievance seems to be that of the still-cleaners. The stills are huge cylindrical vats in which oil, in the process of refining, is subjected to great heat. . . . The heat is intense, estimated usually at 200 degrees Fahrenheit. Only men of the strongest physique can do the work. These men make about $2.25 a day. Yard laborers, who constitute the largest single class of labor, receive $1.75 a day. The bulk of the labor has a nine or ten-hour day though there are some who work twelve hours a day.[74]

On July 20 the entire Standard Oil plant was shut down after the striking still-cleaners persuaded employees from other departments to engage in a sympathy walk-out. By eight o'clock in the morning over 3,000 workers had struck

from virtually every department on the site.[75] Almost immediately strikebreakers were brought onto the scene, and they
were goaded by flagrant racist attitudes engendered by Standard officials in the city. The general manager of the Bayonne
facility instructed the leader of the strikebreakers to "get 250
men who could swing clubs and you can break that strike. If
that's not enough, get 1,000 or 2,000. I want them to break
that strike. I want them to march up East 22 Street and right
through the guts of the Polacks."[76]

Initially the strikers demanded a 15 percent raise, "decent
treatment" at work, and the dismissal of the still-cleaner's fore-
man. Soon, representatives of the International Boilermakers
and Iron Shipbuilder's Union, the Industrial Workers of the
World (IWW), the Central Labor Union of New Jersey, and the
AFL Machinists' Union were in the city to assist the strikers.[77]
However, Standard maintained a firm position not to negotiate.
After consulting with company officials in New York City, the
superintendent of the Bayonne facility announced: "We
absolutely refuse to recognize any man or committee as coming
from a representative of the strikers in our plants. We will only
recognize a written statement as coming from the men of each
department and promise to consider them carefully."[78]

The strikers were equally steadfast. A vote to remain out,
taken in English, Polish, and Italian, produced a unanimous decision to carry on the strike.[79] Eventually, six strikers lost their
lives at the hands of police and company guards. The flames of
violence directed at the strikers were fanned by the press. The
New York Sun advised that the rights of strikers "ended when
they quit work," and referred to those who remained out as
"a crowd of uneducated semi-Americans . . . ignorant of the
English language and all of them unversed in American ideals."[80]
The theme of un-Americanism was pressed by Standard Oil officials when they maintained that many of the strikers were pro-
German, and led by professional agitators who desired to block
the fulfillment of war contracts to the allies. A lawyer who assisted the strikers in writing their demands was accused of being
"an agent of the German Emperor."[81]

The numbers of dead strikers might have been larger had not

the governor of New Jersey refused to call out the militia. The
governor decided not to bring in troops after A. C. Bedford,
then the vice-president of Standard, refused to meet with federal mediators who had arrived in the city. As the governor explained:

> There are three parties to the controversy and not merely
> two as Mr. Bedford seemed to suppose. I reminded him
> that besides the company and the employees the third par-
> ty to the controversy is the public, and the public has
> something to say about the situation. It did not seem to
> me that the vice-president was placing himself and his com-
> pany in the best possible light by rejecting the suggestion
> of arbitration.[82]

Violence against the strikers continued until the sheriff of
Hudson County, Eugene Kinkead, personally intervened to win
the trust of the Standard employees. He arrested the leader of
armed strikebreakers and some company guards. Kinkead explained his actions:

> I wouldn't stand for those armed toughs standing in there
> and shooting. . . . One bullet went through the wall of a
> house where there was a woman and her baby. . . . It's
> got to be understood that these wealthy people with their
> palatial homes can't hire men to shoot down poor people
> just to protect their property. They can't be allowed to
> kill human beings to save mere plants and machinery.[83]

The sheriff was able to convince the men to submit their
wage demands to arbitration, but the company refused any
action until the men quit the strike to return to work.[84] The
strikers were incensed by this turn of events and, the following day, they charged the Tidewater Oil plant which was said
to be a subsidiary of the Standard. When police and guards
opened fire, two strikers were killed.[85]

Kinkead, confronted with adamant positions on both sides
of the conflict, took matters again into his own hands. He

pummeled the leader of the strike committee and Frank Tannenbaum of the IWW with his fists, placed them under arrest, and denounced them to the strikers as traitors to the cause of labor occupied with secret, ulterior motives.[86] The sheriff addressed a mass meeting of strikers and informed them of the alleged treachery of their leaders. He took the speaker's platform, waving an American flag, and promised the workers that he would see to it that they received a wage increase if only they would return to the job. The strikers at the meeting, largely immigrant-workmen, refused the offer.[87] Undaunted, Kinkead gathered a group of American-born strikers in the courthouse and pleaded for concessions. He advised that the leader of the strike had been born in Germany, worked for a socialist newspaper, and was a pro-German propagandist. He ended his impassioned plea before the American audience by exclaiming, "If any man not a citizen here is not satisfied with conditions in this country, in God's name let him go back to the other side."[88]

Inspired by his nativist rhetoric, stunned by the revelations, and pleased with the promise of a wage increase, English-speaking workers began to return to work on July 28. With its leadership either in jail or exiled from the county, the foreign-born workers also returned. The Standard Oil Company eventually did provide increases for the men. Those who had been earning $2.50 a day or less received a 10 percent increase, while all others were provided a twenty-five cent per day increment.[89] In addition, by September the work week was reduced from that of six days of nine hours each to one of six days of eight hours each.[90]

The end of the 1915 strike thus came about with small concessions on the part of the company. Most significantly, the Standard successfully avoided any direct dealings with independent labor organizations. In addition, the sheriff agreed with Standard that no objections would be made against the dismissal of those employees who had opposed "law and order." In reality, that meant that almost every worker who had served on the strike committee or had been active on the picket line was discharged.[91]

However, the situation did not remain peaceful for long.
The Standard Oil plant in Bayonne was shaken by another
strike from October 10 to 20, 1916. The general scenario of
events resembled those of the first strike, and eventually eight
workers lost their lives.[92] From the outset, however, anti-immi-
grant sentiment ran higher than before. Apparently accepting
the company's charges that strikes were the result of professional agitators and the work of foreign, pro-German saboteurs,
the English-speaking workers refused to join in. After checking
for permission with the company, they went so far as to hold
antistrike meetings.[93]

Among the demands of those who did strike were: wage increases, an eight-hour day, twenty minutes for lunch, and hu-
mane treatment "in place of the brutal kicking and punching
we now receive without provocation."[94] Despite the modesty
of the demands strikebreakers were again employed, and the
strikers were portrayed as a wild and ignorant band. The local
press claimed that the strikers were led by "ten-year-old street
urchins" and that the most aggressive of those that had walked
out were "crazed with the drink they have seized."[95] Although
it did not have a reporter on the scene the *New York Globe* ran
the headline, "Bayonne in grip of a commune."[96] So biased
was the press toward the foreign-born strikers that the *New Republic* objected:

> In spite of the fact that the internal evidence of the reports
> themselves makes it clear that the local authorities delib-
> erately adapted a policy of intimidation and violence . . .
> the newspaper headlines were so falsified as to convey the
> impression that they were upholding the law against a
> criminal mob. From the very beginning . . . the Mayor of
> the city announced that he was an attorney for the Stan-
> dard Oil Company and that he approved of the conduct
> of the police.[97]

One reporter who was present in the city wrote that as he
"looked the situation over in Bayonne, it seemed to me that
the issue here is primarily one of Americanism. It is tremen-

dously significant that in the language of the street there are two classes of people in Bayonne—'white' men and foreign- ers."[98] The complaint of a Bayonne businessman was that

> it's a case of the ignorant, low-class foreigner making trouble. . . . This is an orderly, prosperous and com- fortable town. Those fellows live over by themselves and refuse to become Americans. They live in dirt and filth and hoard their money. . . . This is the first time that I have said a good word for the Standard Oil Com- pany, but I am with them on this deal.[99]

During the strike, the socialist press, political leaders, and union organizers were barred from the city. As in 1915, due to the extraordinary violence, federal mediators were called to the scene. Again, however, Standard Oil refused to negoti- ate until the men returned to work. With no apparent alterna- tive, the government conciliators pleaded for the workers to abandon the strike. The strikers, however, did not return, and it was reported that they were interested in joining a union af- filiated with the AFL.[100] The stalemate was broken when 2,000 English-speaking employees were returned to work un- der armed protection.[101] Upon the return of the mass of work- ers, the local press opined:

> This condition was created by the unlicensed and un- bridled activities of perhaps not more than 300 discon- tented foreign-born and foreign-speaking workers, who were doubtless inspired to their activities by a heredi- tary impulse to wreck and ruin when the restraints of their native environment were changed to the wide free- dom found in their new homes in America. Their acts during the strike . . . [were] due to ignorance or lack of the knowledge of self-government.[102]

It is probable that John Commons would have agreed with the above editorial. But, as noted earlier, big business inter- preted Commons's labor theory in its own way. If necessary, union challenges to corporate autonomy were to be crushed by force. Corporate America agreed that foreign-born workers were in need of education, but not of the type that would be forthcoming from participation in independent unions. Work-ers were to be educated according to the terms dictated by the company. Ten months prior to the 1916 Bayonne strike John D. Rockefeller, Jr., unveiled his plan for an "industrial constitution" (i.e., the Standard Oil variant of company union-ism), proclaiming:

> Some have spoken of it as establishing a Republic of La-bor. Certain it is that the plan gives every employee op-portunity to voice his complaints and aspirations, and it neglects no occasion to bring the men and the managers together to talk over their common interests. . . . This plan is not hostile to labor organizations . . . neither mem-bership in a union nor independence of a union will bring a man either preference or reproach.[103]

The Standard Oil workers of Bayonne learned the conse-quences of expressing their interests when they were not com-mon to "the men and the managers together." The 1915 and 1916 Standard Oil strikes were also a harbinger of things to come for relations between big businessmen and their employ-ees. Oil company charges that strikers were ignorant immi-grants goaded by unscrupulous union organizers, professional agitators, saboteurs, and pro-German agents were replicated in the steel industry strike of 1919. The only change was that pro-German was rendered as pro-Bolshevik. Once the label was applied the use of terror and violence to protect corporate au-tonomy was executed and justified before the public.

As is evident from the consideration of the Bayonne strikes, the atmosphere that permitted the "red scare" and the destruc-tion of the labor movement existed before there was a Bolshe-vik revolution in Russia. In essence, that atmosphere was pro-duced by big business committed to retain its autonomy at the work site.

> The very wording of Jersey's [Standard Oil] public statements was that employed by other businessmen faced with identical situations in other companies

and in other industries. It is indeed remarkable how
homogeneous were American managerial attitudes toward labor situations at this time.[104]

Corporate America, since the turn of the century, had
adapted a variety of welfare measures for its workers. Big
business, by 1916, was experimenting with company unionism. If American workers were motivated primarily by economistic motives, then surely such advances would satisfy them.
The widespread strikes in oil and steel revealed that this line
of thought was flawed. To the new economic elite of the nation, as for the labor theory of John Commons, the problem
was to be found in the ignorant, uneducated immigrant mass.

Yet, businessmen charged that the masses were prodded on
by pro-German or pro-Bolshevik agents and a variety of un-
American agitators. For workers led and inspired by types such
as these, the only effective teacher was force. One important
reason for the influence of this corporate perspective on capital
and labor relations was that it represented a relatively clear and
coherent view. In contrast, by 1918, the view of the federal
government was confused and contradictory. The various
branches of government flashed differing signals to interested
observers:

> At the very moment when the U.S. Supreme Court was
> preparing an opinion which restrained labor in its work
> of trade union organization, when the Postmaster-Gen-
> eral was calling upon congress to revoke the act of 1912
> permitting the unionization of federal employees. . . .
> The President's Mediation Commission . . . was imposing
> collective bargaining upon the copper mines of Arizona.[105]

Big businessmen in America could envision caring for their
employees through welfare capitalist programs and talking with
their workers in company unions. What they could not imagine
was surrendering even a shred of autonomy to independently
organized unions of working people. It was this lack of imagination that necessitated businessmen's own interpretations of
Commons's labor theory. In fact, the old middle-class assump-

tions behind his ideas rendered Commons's theory naive. The full implications of this situation were evident in an article written for the *American Journal of Sociology* by an official of a large manufacturing corporation early in 1916:

> Democracy would not triumph if "unionism" as now interpreted should prevail. The latter would be an oligarchy of a most selfish and relentless type. The true democracy demands fair treatment for all and a division of opportunity and reward commensurate with each man's ability. This ideal may never be fully realized, but it cannot even be approximated until all feelings of antagonism are subdued and a spirit of co-operation and good-will predominates. Early action is imperative, and the initiative should be taken by the employer. The present condition of affairs cannot continue without jeopardizing, not only the welfare, but also the very existence of our institutions.[106]

9 Institutionalization of Commons-Wisconsin Theory

IT IS SOMETIMES SAID THAT BUSINESSMEN in America were unconcerned with, or ignorant of, social scientific thought. Such opinions, however, are unfounded. As Edward Kirkland noted with regard to the sentiments within the business community near the turn of the century:

> The more articulate of business leaders and of course their spokesmen showed an acquaintance with the English classical school and with contemporary English and continental economic thought. . . . Businessmen in their dilemmas were not content to rely upon a political economy drawn from the past. A large number joined hands with some reformers after the Civil War in an active program to develop and refine social science. . . . An examination of the attitudes of this business generation toward certain, but not all, social, political and economic issues faces the handicap of silence on the part of some . . . and the lack of systematic thought and expression on the part of others. This fact has sometimes been made to carry the implication that the business community was too barbaric to think about what it was doing or not literate enough to put it down on paper. This charge is ludicrous.[1]

Indeed, men of business were not reticent about their opinions of some reformers within the social sciences. As a nineteenth-century Boston businessman complained,

"Who are the men engaged in promulgating these so-called
reforms, ostensibly for the benefit of workingmen? Are
they not for the most part theorists with unbalanced minds?"[2]
A contributor to the *American Journal of Sociology* apparently agreed with the businessman's critique:

> It must be admitted that this rigorous protest . . . is
> not without justification. Social theorists need to be
> meek men, and should stand with their head uncovered
> before the special gifts and services of the men of genius
> who are working the latter day miracles of industry and
> commerce.[3]

And the "gifts and services" bestowed upon educational institutions by "the men of genius" were indeed plentiful. As one
historian noted, "Hand in hand with the dollar, the businessmen
marched into the potential control room of Academe . . .
[boards of trustees were filled by] businessmen, bankers and
lawyers."[4] The National Association of Manufacturers actively
sought to impress its views upon the university world. Officials
of the organization addressed a variety of academic groups and
exerted pressure for the appointment of two of its favored professors to a federal commission on industrial relations.[5]

The captains of industry had begun to invest heavily in the
maintenance and advancement of university education in the
United States during the 1890s. Ideas concerning the social responsibilities of the wealthy grew in importance near the end of
the nineteenth century. As Frederick Rudolph noted, "The application of Darwinian social analysis to the meaning of his own
life led Andrew Carnegie to devote a great fortune to the benefit of mankind, and it prompted much of the benefaction that
underwrote the university era."[6] In addition, by funding colleges and universities men such as Carnegie and J. D. Rockefeller
believed that they were helping to preserve American social institutions. [7]

The expanding universities in the nation increasingly sought
to attract the favor of wealthy businessmen as potential donors.[8]
College administrators thus became concerned with public relations; anything that jeopardized the favors of contributors was

considered an abomination. In essence, the passions of prospective contributors came to influence the attitudes of university personnel. [9] As Laurence Veysey explained, "The history of academic freedom in America thus became a rather accurate reflection of the degree of social alarm felt at any given hour by the more substantial elements in the American population."[10] Though, in general, it would be unreasonable to assert that wealthy contributors directly controlled the faculties, it was the case that their influence was felt through the governing boards of educational institutions. [11] So great did the influence of businessmen on university boards of trustees become that some people wondered whether schools would become identical to business corporations:

> The American university, whether supported by private gift or by the State, is conducted under an administrative system which approximates closer and closer as time goes on to that of a business corporation. The administrative power is lodged in a small body of trustees or regents, who are not members of the university community. . . . The board of trustees, even in our older colleges and universities, is chosen almost entirely from businessmen and on the basis of business experience. It is no longer considered necessary that the president should be a scholar. The board of trustees, with the president as its chief executive officer, passes upon the entire policy and administration of the institution.[12]

In some cases, however, direct control over faculties did occur. For example, Frederick Jackson Turner explained that the board of regents at the University of Wisconsin "used to sit with a red lead pencil in consultation over the lists of books submitted by professors, and strike out those that failed to please their fancy."[13] In a similar vein, Mrs. Leland Stanford had E. A. Ross dismissed from the university bearing her husband's name because she did not care for the prolabor statements issued by the professor.[14] The Ross case proved to be particularly controversial. Henry Carter Adams refused to sign a report by the American Economics Association regarding the incident "as a means of stating to the working people of the United States that the economists had not been bought."[15]

Adams's opinion was not unopposed. When queried as to what material should be taught by social scientists in the universities a trustee of Northwestern University, an officer of the Western Railroad Association, replied that professors

> should promptly and gracefully submit it to the determination of the trustees when the latter find it necessary to act. . . . If the trustees err it is for the patrons and proprietors, not for the employees, to change either the policy or the personnel of the board.[16]

Almost unanimous opinion was voiced in favor of the above sentiment by members of the boards of trustees at the universities of Chicago, Columbia, Princeton, Yale, Johns Hopkins, Pennsylvania, and American.[17] By 1905 Charles Eliot, the president of Harvard University, publicly applauded employer attacks against labor unions. [18]

It was by virtue of the restrictive circumstances described above that interpretations of the labor movement in America with which business benefactors could not sympathize gradually were filtered from the academic scene. In 1894 alone, the year of the famous Pullman strike, a significant number of renowned scholars either were dismissed or condemned for their unacceptable views by university boards of regents. [19] The fates that befell Richard Ely and Henry Carter Adams already have been documented in earlier chapters. The influence of university benefactors, direct and indirect, was so great that by the early part of this century dissident interpreters of the labor movement had been removed from or silenced within the academies. This fact was of great importance in that the interpretations of Ely and Adams represented the greatest source of competition for the Commons-Wisconsin theory.[20] Once other voices of reform had been restrained Commons's ideas came to enjoy a premier place among university-based theories of labor.

By 1915 business attempts to influence universities had spread still further. In Wisconsin a legislative proposal was offered to

reorganize the facilities of higher education under the central-
ized control of three businessmen appointed by the governor.
Retrenchment and administration on lines of "efficiency" were
demanded by state officials. [21] Thus, another significant consequence of the financial support of universities by men of business was a call for the modernization and rationalization of the
system of higher education. What this meant was that, aside
from upgrading faculties and curricula, efficiency of operations
became a valued quality.[22] In short, the businessman's perspective became significant in organizing academic life. This contributed to a "rationalized" academic division of labor. Indirectly,
this virtually assured a paramount position within the university for Commons's interpretation of the labor movement. To
avoid duplication of effort Commons was given free reign to
formulate historical-theoretical studies of American labor. Other scholars interested in labor were to content themselves with
more topical studies.

Evidence suggests that George Barnett, who became known
for his studies of the effects of mechanization upon workers,
explicitly agreed not to infringe upon Commons's area of concern—the interpretation of the labor movement.[23] A recognition of this academic division of labor was evident in the efforts
of other contemporary, university-based scholars. Jacob Hol-
lander, Robert Hoxie, and Carleton Parker all concentrated
upon more microcosmic and more practical studies of labor.[24]
By the 1920s, then, the Commons-Wisconsin theory of labor in
America did enjoy a rather unique and favored place within the
universities. The Commons-Wisconsin theory thereby became
institutionalized as the acceptable academic interpretation of
the labor movement.

Although the status of Commons was bolstered by the trend
toward efficiency, other academics expressed resentment. Demands for efficiency within the universities were opposed by
some. As one professor complained in the pages of *The Nation:*

> Businessmen frequently tell scholars what they think of
> them, and sometimes favor them with their advice, very
> often with their money. The scholar then becomes the
> employee. . . . Frankly, then, I am tired of scientific man-

agement, so-called. . . . Shall scholars then continue to look with equanimity upon the management of our universities by businessmen under the application of business criteria of efficiency? Heaven forbid![25]

Also voicing discontent with the advancing business infringement upon university operations was a college president, W. T. Foster, who wrote:

Certain professors have been refused reelection lately, apparently because they set their students to thinking in ways objectionable to the trustees. It would be well if more teachers were dismissed because they fail to stimulate thinking of any kind. . . . It is better for students to think about heresies than not to think at all.[26]

The *New York Times* heartily disagreed with the philosophy of education espoused by president Foster:

Men who through toil and ability have got together enough money to endow universities or professors' chairs do not generally have it in mind that their money should be spent for the dissemination of the dogmas of Socialism. . . . Yet when Trustees conscientiously endeavor to carry out the purposes of the founder by taking proper measures to prevent the misuse of the endowment, we always have a loud howl about academic freedom. We can see no reason why the upholders of academic freedom in that sense should not establish a university of their own.[27]

Some big businessmen were not content to exercise indirect control over intellectuals. Rather, they sought to bring them directly into their employ. John D. Rockefeller, Jr., for example, put W. L. MacKenzie King, a former Canadian secretary of labor, in charge of the Rockefeller Foundation inquiry into industrial relations. Wrote Rockefeller in his recommendation of King:

> Mr. King is a man who has approached this subject from
> both the theoretical and practical side . . . [His success in
> Canada] was due partly to his extensive knowledge and
> wide experience in dealing with industrial difficulties and
> partly to the fact that he has the faculty of making men
> of high and low degree believe in his sincerity and genu-
> ineness.[28]

Mr. King apparently instructed Rockefeller along lines which
the latter appreciated. In August 1914, King indicated that labor's demands for autonomy would be rendered but a "shadow"
issue:

> In certain industries it is going to be easy for employers
> to find all the labor they desire, and unions will be con-
> fronted with a new problem. Recognition, simply for the
> sake of recognition, is going to be seen less pressing as an
> immediate end, than that of maintaining standards already
> existing, and may rightly come to regard as their friends
> and allies companies and corporations large enough and
> fair enough to desire to maintain these standards of their
> own accord. For the unions to take a different view will
> certainly mean to lose the substance of fair conditions
> while wasting resources in fighting for the shadow of rec-
> ognition.[29]

Writing a few years earlier, Andrew Carnegie, too, expressed
optimism regarding the eventual development of the relations
between capital and labor:

> Co-partnership tends to bring a realizing sense of truth to
> both labor and capital that their interests, broadly con-
> sidered, are mutual. . . . Given a just system of taxation
> and a system of partnership between labor and capital,
> and there is no assignable limit to the progress of the
> worker. . . . Never have the masses made such rapid and
> substantial progress as in recent years. . . . With their
> trades unions, cash payments—masters of themselves and
> their labors—it is clear that workingmen have shared in

the general advance. The wand of progress has not passed them by untouched, nor are we without evidence that the march of their improvement is not to stop.[30]

Carnegie's optimism for the tendencies within the evolutionary process also found expression in his Foundation for the Advancement of Teaching. It seemed as if the foundation was to help the process of evolution along. The operation of the foundation attempted to assure that " strong and ambitious men" would be drawn to the intellectual life for the betterment of society. One report noted that few professors "receive a sufficient sum of money to support a family and make provision for old age." The report claimed that this situation must be corrected "if strong and ambitious men are to be drawn in sufficient numbers."[31] The funds made available by Carnegie were administered by a board of trustees composed of three businessmen and twenty-two presidents of colleges and universities.[32] Indeed, this was the way Carnegie intended things to be done. As he expressed it, "Americans put their money under the control of business men at the head of the universities."[33]

Given the attitudes of significant numbers of the officials of postsecondary educational institutions in the United States (see earlier portions of this chapter), it is safe to assume that the Carnegie funds were controlled by the hands of businessmen, and by academics sympathetic to their values and beliefs. The evidence suggests that John Commons was the type of "strong and ambitious man" to be favored by the benefactors of higher education.

Of all the labor theories only that of John Commons attracted the financial support of big business. As a consequence of that support, only the thoughts of John Commons were buttressed by the resources which eventually permitted his ideas to develop into a "school" of labor theory.

What rendered Commons's ideas unobjectionable to the captains of industry cum benefactors? His theory reproduced essential elements of their own ideology. That Commons's work was financed directly by the donations of Andrew Carnegie is not surprising in that the social outlooks of the two men dovetailed almost perfectly. First, Commons and Carnegie agreed that

America was basically a land of opportunity wherein the ambitious individual could advance himself.[34] They agreed on the essential features of the American political and social systems. Second, Commons and Carnegie agreed that education was the most valuable means of enculturating immigrants to American ideals and institutions. Education was the key to the maintenance of democracy.[35] Third, both men denounced monopolies (neither saw anything wrong with a business merely because it was of a large scale) and were wary of financial speculators.[36] Finally, Commons's insistence on purely voluntary negotiations between capital and labor did not challenge Carnegie's pragmatic attitudes toward the labor movement. In Carnegie's view, labor was sometimes to be bargained with and sometimes repressed. Which policy was followed depended upon the contingencies of the moment.[37] As revealed by the history of the relations between capital and labor in the 1900 to World War I period (see chapter 8) this view was shared by a significant number of American businessmen. The outlook of Rockefeller, a heavy contributor to the University of Chicago, was basically the same as that of Carnegie.[38] Given the similarities between the views of Commons and Carnegie, it is understandable that the latter's money could fund the research of the former in full confidence.[39]

Yet, specific point of agreement between Commons and Carnegie, by themselves, merely allude to the most significant explanation for the affinity of the two men for each other. The most important fact is that John Commons, Carnegie, and the big businessmen of the early twentieth century shared similar beliefs and values, as well as some interests. In short, they tended to be most comfortable with the assumptions and culture of the traditional middle class. This is essential for an appreciation of the relationship between Commons and his benefactors:

> The modern scientific community has been credited with an ethos which reduces social influences upon the production and reception of knowledge claims to a minimum, thereby guaranteeing the accumulation of objective knowledge. . . . [But] it is preferable to think of scientific

knowledge as a contingent cultural product, which cannot
be separated from the social context in which it is produced. . . . Scientists today still make considerable use of
commonsense knowledge which is acquired largely in the
course of non-scientific activities . . . commonsense modes
of perception and operation are an integral and essential
feature of recognized scientific practice.[40]

Business encouragement for Commons's efforts clearly was
important. However, that support cannot provide the full explanation for the recognition afforded to the theory that
emerged at Wisconsin. That is, the Commons-Wisconsin approach had an appeal due to its own merits. Although labor
research was conducted at other schools, students were attracted to the style of the efforts underway at Wisconsin. As
Paul McNulty noted, "It is not simply that the University of
Wisconsin was the leading center for labor studies; the temper
of the Wisconsin approach attracted and was characteristic of
many other leading students of labor."[41] Above all, that "temper" reflected efforts at theoretical as well as social, political,
and economic reform in an era when the rapid maturation of
industrial capitalism introduced severe problems and disloca-
tions to American society.[42]

The above point cannot be overlooked when considering
the reception granted to the Commons-Wisconsin theory. The
theoretical approach generated by Commons had emerged
from the new political economy as part of an effort to transcend a theoretical orthodoxy which appeared irrelevant in
light of the great social changes that had occurred in the United States. To many young scholars, the labor research conducted at other institutions did not seem as interesting or as
relevant. For example, the work done on labor at Johns Hopkins University was much more closely integrated with orthodox theoretical positions, and far less reformist in its tendencies,
when compared to the efforts conducted under Commons.[43]
Business interests did have more money than others to invest in
people and ideas that they liked.[44] This, of course, was relevant
in the case of Commons. Ultimately, however, those interests

did not control the reactions of others to the research generated at Wisconsin. Commons's work spoke for reform, and this is what made it attractive to many in academia.

Despite the inability of interested parties to control reaction to the ideas in which they had invested, it is unwise to discount the significance of the support that was forthcoming for Commons's work in its early stages. Support, be it material, moral, or both, often is crucial to a researcher. When it is lacking, promising new lines of inquiry and thought remain just that—promises which never attain fulfillment. In this regard, the role of the theorist may be likened to that of the artist. With this analogy in mind, the following comments may be instructive:

> The situation of a gifted artist who neither consciously nor unconsciously reveals kinship with the dominant taste is not a comfortable one. Many such artists are foredoomed to failure . . . of those who in their hearts want to go other ways, most will find no opportunity of expressing themselves, or will soon be silenced.[45]

The application of these thoughts to the labor theorists is apparent when the fates of Ely and Adams are recalled. Their theoretical efforts did not satisfy the tastes of would-be benefactors, and they were not the recipients of the kinds of support provided to Commons. Ultimately, then, special interests could neither create labor theory nor control the reactions to that which was produced, but, by providing support for some views and not others, businessmen could either encourage or discourage lines of inquiry. Commons, by borrowing from the valuable ideas of his predecessors, was able to formulate a theory that was of particular appeal to influential and interested parties. His version of labor theory was encouraged. Thus, while it was not the case that powerful interests created the new theory, they were influential enough to mark the avenues along which inquiry proceeded free from detours.

Businessmen, however, were not the only group to perceive an affinity with the Commons theory of labor. Support for the ideas and philosophy inherent in the Commons-Wisconsin

approach also existed within the leadership stratum of the
AFL. In line with the Commons emphasis on purely voluntary
agreements between labor and capital, the AFL convention
proceedings for 1920 recorded:

> In the demand for collective bargaining labor has never
> asked that it be gained by law. It must come through . . .
> evolution in the minds of employers, who will be induced
> to accept it because of its advantages.[46]

Opposition to competing ideas became particularly vehement
among the AFL officials during the years following World War
I. As one historian suggested, the behavior of the AFL president, "showed how thoroughly his once militant determination to organize all American workers had given way to an ob-
session with the survival of his cherished craft unions and the
preservation of his own reputation."[47] The postwar defeats of
labor removed the edge from internal opposition to official
AFL doctrine and policy.[48] Leaders of the labor organization,
however, were not content to have a diminished opposition.
They brooked no differences at all. Indeed, those within the
AFL who still hoped to organize the largely immigrant workers in the mass production industries, and in the process bring
about the creation of industrial unions, were denounced as
communist-inspired.[49] Here, it is useful to recall that it was
the Commons theory that suggested that immigrant workers
were particularly prone to radical notions of one sort or
another. Gompers and the AFL leadership could find the theory particularly useful in defeating their opponents inside the
labor movement.

Other supporters of ideas drawn from the Commons-Wisconsin theory were encouraged by what transpired within labor. In
fact, they hoped to go still further. Ralph Easley of the NCF,
himself an early proponent of Commons's work, wrote in 1920
that "since the labor movement was organizing to fight the
IWW and the bolsheviki, the NCF should undertake to clean
them out from the churches, the colleges, the universities, and
the various places which the labor movement could not reach."[50]

Gompers and the conservative officialdom of the AFL supported Easley no less strongly than did leading industrialists.[51] The postwar hysteria did have more than a temporary effect:

> The underlying fear of radicalism and the proclivity for intolerance which the Red Scare had engendered remained long after. . . . In fact, the antiradical emotionalism emanating from the scare affected both governmental and private thinking for almost a decade. . . .
>
> For a time at least, no one dared live on the bright mountain top of intellectual curiosity. . . . While teachers on all levels of instruction retained the theoretical right to free speech, they were abject fools if they exercised it.[52]

One of the disheartening effects of the red scare was still greater inhibitions on the development of new or alternative ideas in labor theory. By 1920, events showed that the Commons-Wisconsin theory deserved to be scrutinized more carefully. However, the chill of reaction was felt within the universities. Indeed, even Commons was not above the suspicion of some of the "patriotic" organizations that surfaced in the wake of World War I.[53] Ideas that challenged Commons's version of labor theory were afforded refuge for a time in educational institutions connected to the labor movement. Unfortunately, there, too, blocks were erected against thought that argued with what had become official doctrine.

The situation that developed in labor's own institutions was especially distressing in that one reason for their creation was the lack of freedom that characterized other educational structures. As the bylaws for the Brookwood Labor College stated:

> Teachers are to be accorded the fullest possible freedom to investigate and set forth the truth, since it is clearly undesirable that a school carried on under the auspices of the labor movement and serving that movement should fall into the same error of suppressing freedom of thought and expression which both the labor movement and intel-

ligent educationalists deplore in the case of other institutions of learning.[54]

During the 1920s AFL officials assumed censorship control over the publications of the Workers Education Bureau (WEB), a group formed by trade unionists and scholars to coordinate the educational efforts of organized labor. Included among the complaints of AFL leaders against the WEB publications were charges that they criticized craft organization, approved the formation of a labor party, and advocated the nationalization of industry along with some form of workers' control. Officials within the AFL also brought about the disaffiliation of unions from Brookwood Labor College on the grounds that all of its faculty members were "left-wing," and "radical doctrines" were taught in every class.[55] Clearly, among the serious setbacks suffered by labor in the 1920s were included some inflicted by its own hand.

The disappearance of formal opposition to leadership policy and ideology within the AFL was accompanied by great losses in union membership.[56] Due to these factors, as well as the outright repression visited upon workers, there no longer existed an independent, militant, and organized labor movement of significant size in the United States. The consequences of this were important for labor theory. Since the days of Ely, labor theory sought to provide an understanding of the labor movement in America. Indeed, labor theorists had taken the existence of the movement to be synonymous with "the labor problem." Postwar developments, however, had removed the problem by virtually destroying the movement. Moreover, subsequent events appeared to corroborate the Commons view that American labor was essentially conservative and job-conscious. For example, the leaders of what remained of the AFL began to express an interest in cooperating with the company unions that became widespread during the 1920s. In addition, throughout the decade the Federation sold advertising space in its journal to businesses that maintained company unions or operated with an open-shop policy.[57]

Scholars interested in labor altered their focus to keep abreast of social developments. Due, in part, to the events noted above, there was a shift in interest from labor problems to a more narrow labor economics. Attention increasingly was focused on industrial relations in an era that witnessed advances in the techniques of scientific management and the growth of company unionism.[58] Labor theory, in the sense afforded it by the efforts of Ely, Adams, and Commons, ceased to exist when the object of its analysis no longer remained as a problem to be understood. It is ironic that the most renowned of labor theories, the Commons-Wisconsin version, attained the greatest recognition and acceptance only with destruction of the very thing it sought to explain—an independent, organized labor movement in America.

John Commons and his benefactors and supporters never appreciated fully the significance for labor of the issue of autonomy. It was the autonomy issue which constantly pitted the forces of capital and labor against each other. Big businessmen simply refused to cede any of their autonomy in the workplace and, in fact, actively sought to increase their control of the work process. Although Commons's labor theory called for the recognition of unions, his plea always was relative, a means to an end —to thwart the increase of socialist sympathies within the American working class. Never did it appear as an end in itself.

As was the case with many traditional middle-class intellectuals who grew to maturity in the late nineteenth century, John Commons began his career within the Social Gospel movement. Some theorists who had studied abroad, such as Richard Ely and Henry Carter Adams, were able to transcend their sociocultural backgrounds to some extent. For Commons, however, the basic outlook which he derived from an early involvement with Christian Socialism remained with him. Labor historians have noted that "labor was committed to mass action, a point social gospellers never understood in the same way that workers did. In the final analysis, most social gospellers fell back upon individualism and had little faith in such action."[59]

In sum, then, the Commons-Wisconsin theory proved suitable to the interests of some businessmen by virtue of its thesis of American exceptionalism as it served to validate a belief in the viability of the nation's political-economic structure.

Likewise, the theory bolstered the interests of leaders within the AFL who doubted the worthiness of the immigrant workers in the mass-production industries. In addition, Commons tended to look more favorably upon the large corporation than did earlier labor theorists.[60] When the inadequacy of his explanation for the development of radicalism and socialist sympathies among American workers is recalled, it is clear that an affinity with the values and perspective of business interests, and the interests of labor bureaucrats in the AFL, is the most significant factor in accounting for the acceptability and eventual popularity of Commons's theory. The ideas of earlier theorists whose works shared less or no affinity with the special interests, but which did provide more adequate explanations for the existence of radicalism and militancy among organized workers, gradually faded from public consciousness.[61]

It was some time ago that the complaint was heard that serious scholarship had yet to come to grips with the ideology of John Commons: "We can no longer ignore Commons as a sedate and non-controversial scholar; and no longer view his interpretation of American labor history as a movement of a sedate and non-controversial scholarship."[62] Perhaps this study may represent an initial step toward the fulfillment of that hope

10 Conclusion _____

THE ANALYSIS IN THIS BOOK DEMONSTRATES that Richard
Ely, Henry Carter Adams, and John Commons were prompted
to concern with the emergence of the labor movement in the
United States by virtue of the threats they perceived against
middle-class values. In essence, the work of all three theorists
was motivated by the same intention: to reform American
capitalism in order to enable it to cope with the challenges of
socialism and militant labor.

John Commons's interpretation of the labor movement is
the most widely accepted today. Yet, this study has shown
his explanation for the existence of radicalism within the labor
movement to be inadequate. The data examined in this work
demonstrated that the political sympathies of organized workers were associated with the social conditions of industry rather
than an assumed uniqueness of American society. However, the
acceptability of a theory may be determined on grounds other
than the weight of evidence used to support it. As shown in this
study, this was the case with the theory of John Commons.

There was a great effort in the late nineteenth and early twentieth centuries for change in the realm of social thought. Traditional theories were revealed as inadequate to make sense of the
social developments introduced by the rapid maturation of industrial capitalism. Efforts at reform, whether in theory or society, did not occur in a vacuum. Indeed, the realm of theory that
spoke to "the labor problem" touched upon a subject which
was of vital, practical concern to the interests of powerful
groups in the American political-economic system. Businessmen

often brought pressure to bear upon the scholars who addressed the situation of the labor movement. In fact, all of the young men concerned with labor theory experienced difficulties in their careers for advancing views which were suspect. Only the theory promulgated by John Commons eventually received encouragement from powerful and interested parties.

While men of wealth could not control the forces that gave rise to the emergence of labor theory, they could bring pressures to bear on the directions that theory took. If the movement for reform in theory could not be prevented, powerful interests could mark the intellectual limits beyond which danger lurked. By their support, businessmen suggested that the Commons version of labor theory did not transcend their sense of respectability. E. P. Thompson described the consequences of this process of influence:

> Intellectuals may be employed, promoted, neglected in ratio to their acceptability to ruling interests. Few are silenced by force and few are bought outright; but fewer still can resist the 'natural' economic processes and pressures to conform.[1]

The behavior of the leadership bureaucracy within the AFL during the postwar years appeared to provide some corroboration for the Commons-Wisconsin theory. Yet, this was but an appearance. The "live and let live" policy that Commons had projected for relations between capital and labor came to pass only after the life of the labor movement was extinguished in a wave of repression. In essence, Commons's interpretation of the labor movement in America became a refuge for labor leaders with no one left to lead.

The reasons for the continued popularity of Commons's ideas beyond the second decade of the century are twofold. The nature of the social context in which Commons worked provides part of the explanation. John Commons lived in a world that was witnessing the decline of the traditional middle class. While Commons sought to combat this trend, his service on state and federal government commissions and advisory boards only contributed to the development of one aspect of the trend he abhorred—statism and bureaucratic government.[2] As Robert Wiebe indicated:

> [1916] marked the completion of the federal scientific establishment; covering industry, agriculture and an assortment of public services. . . . Agencies accumulated their files and procedures and precedents. . . . Entering the war, the leaders of America's rudimentary bureaucracy were still conditioned to fight the battles of twenty years before. . . . New problems generated in the course of solving old ones fell largely beyond their set visions.[3]

Acting in the interest of a social group which was already in decline, the actions Commons set upon proved to be counterproductive. The nascent bureaucracy of which he was a part was shortly to be manned and fine-tuned by men with outlooks different from his own. The agencies of the government would soon be employed not only to combat militancy and socialism within labor but, in addition, to bring about the formation of a State-managed corporate form of capitalism.

In this sense, the State-initiated labor measures of the New Deal appear to corroborate the analysis and the validity of the proposals put forth by Henry Carter Adams. Yet, it was the theory of Commons that continued to enjoy the greatest amount of popularity and acceptance.[4] The reason for this was that the theory of John Commons possessed an affinity with the interests of the new Statist-capitalist elite. It could continue to serve as a validation of the fundamental viability and legitimacy of the American political-economic system.[5]

The continued popularity of Commons's ideas beyond the 1920s may also be accounted for by the efforts of his students. It was the work of those students, building upon the monopolistic advantage that Commons's theory enjoyed, which transformed the Commons-Wisconsin ideas into the ideas of the Wisconsin School. Through Selig Perlman and, later, Philip Taft, Commons's interpretation of American labor was carried into the 1960s.[6] Though these scholars introduced revisions into the ideas of their master, the essence of Commons's theory was preserved.[7]

The findings of this work possess implications relevant to the contemporary critical treatment of the Commons-Wisconsin theory and early American sociology. Critical analysts have treated the Commons-Wisconsin theory as if it were little more than a rationalization of narrow economic interests. Thus, for example, Philip Foner suggested that the Commons-Wisconsin School was an apologia for Gompersism.[8] Similarly, Michael Rogin and Gary Fink, in separate analyses, suggested that the ideas expressed in Commons's theory were the ideas most useful to the interests of officials and bureaucrats within the AFL and the larger craft unions.[9] These critics tend to confuse the intentions of Commons with those who saw their own uses for his ideas.

By recognizing that a common basis for those theorists who contributed to the development of the Commons-Wisconsin theory was traditional middle-class values, it becomes clear that one is dealing with much more than an apologia or defense of narrow economic interests. Also, one is dealing with thought not labeled easily as either liberal or conservative.[10] It is in this regard that the voices of John Commons, Richard Ely, and Henry Carter Adams must also be understood as having been raised to preserve what they took to constitute the rudiments of democracy. Given the traditional middle-class belief of a "balance theory" of democratic society, the arguments for workers' rights in the form of bargaining should be viewed as containing two thrusts.[11] That one thrust was to combat socialism and militant labor was documented in this study.

The other thrust of this early sociological thought was directed at preventing the rise of despotism in industrial society which, the theorists feared, might be brought about by the emergence of large-scale, monopolistic industrial enterprises and a bureaucratic state. It is true that early labor theory represented a battle against socialism. Yet, it also represented a struggle for the traditional middle-class notion of democracy.[12] That this other thrust was intended to provide for some neutral balance point in society is evident especially in Commons's disinterest in legalistic or bureaucratic solutions to the labor problem. In this focus, too, Commons's thought betrayed an association with the values and assumptions of the traditional middle class. Indeed, for Commons bureaucratic solutions were representative of but another attempt to secure "an exclusive possession of power."[13] He preferred solution through a method of "administration" since:

> The legislative method treats all employers alike as criminals, and forces all to combine and to support the same lobbyists, in order to resist what they consider destructive laws. The administrative method permits the leading representatives of employers to consult with the representatives of labor and with the officials who represent the state, regarding all of the details necessary to carry the law into effect and to adjust it to all conditions. The method is practically that of the voluntary joint conference of collective bargaining. The process is educational and cooperative rather than argumentative and coercive.[14]

Just as Commons always sought to bar outside advisors to labor from the kind of proceedings described above, so he advised the same with regard to the side of capital. In fact, Commons wanted among employer representatives neither financial or commercial interests, but, rather, "men in charge of production who have grown up in the industry and know the labor conditions."[15] When it came to actual negotiation between labor and capital, Commons wanted only those directly involved with production to have a part. If Commons's traditional middle-class mentality brought him to distrust proponents of socialism and militancy for labor, it also inspired him to be wary of all but those close to the entrepreneurial ranks within business.

Middle-class ideology also brought Commons to view the State as a neutral agency whose task it was to provide a setting within which there could transpire an educational process supervised by learned people who, like himself, had the interests of society in mind. Commons believed that such men could provide the balance which he viewed as so crucial to the perpetuation of a democratic system. It is because of this view that an argument may be made that the work of Commons represented an early indicator of the emergence of a "New Class" in the United States.[16] Although this line of thought may possess a certain truth, it can be advanced only with extreme caution. If it is not done so, then one is likely to commit yet again the error of confounding the project of the theorist with that of others. In brief, as Commons's theory could be used by the businessmen and labor bureaucrats of his own day to advance their special interests, so it could later be used by a Statist-capitalist elite. As noted previously, that Commons's thought could be so employed was one reason for the continued popularity of the Commons-Wisconsin theory. Ultimately, however, it is crucial to remember that seldom if ever is a social theory representative of "nothing but" the purposes for which would-be supporters employ it.

Given the manner in which tradtional middle-class ideology was uncritically incorporated into his theory, Commons's thought may accurately be considered as naive.[17] Yet, it is going rather too far to claim that his theoretical efforts were largely "meaningless and irrelevant."[18] To advance such a proposition suggests only that one has refused to take Commons's project or its ramifications seriously. The form of society he sought to preserve certainly was meaningful to the middle class of the early twentieth century. That Commons's project may no longer make sense to our contemporary thinkers simply indicates how far social developments have taken us from the milieu of the early sociological theorists.

As indicated at the beginning of the present work, sociological analysis of the work of the early American sociologists have been few and far between. The studies that do exist tend either to focus on the same relatively few early sociologists or on a general overview of the development of sociology in the United States.[19] One consequence is that it is difficult to formulate anything but rather general statements regarding the early sociologists and significant differences between the scholars are obscured. Thus, for example, the Hinkles relate that American sociologists prior to 1920 had strong rural and religious backgrounds, came from the midwest and were interested in the social problems connected with industrialization.[20] The liabilities of this type of generalization are most evident in the recent work of some sociologists who have taken a critical view of early sociology in America.

Dusky Lee Smith and Herman and Julia Schwendinger agree that the early sociologists "were ideal protagonists for corporate capitalism."[21] The findings of this study suggest that such general statements are misleading. As demonstrated earlier, of the ideas of the early labor theorists, only those of John Commons were deemed worthy of support by influential business interests in the early twentieth century. For this reason it is not valid to conclude that early sociologists were ideal protagonists for corporate capitalism. Since corporate interests rejected the ideas of Richard Ely and Henry Carter Adams, and even those of Commons for a time, one can only infer that their ideas were judged to be less than ideal.

Early sociologists in America were interested in a panoply of problems; to name but a few, the labor movement, crime and delinquency, immigration, pauperism, and race relations. My study has focused only on those sociologists whose work was heavily concerned with the labor movement. Similar studies concerned with the efforts of scholars interested in other problem areas can clarify further the work of early sociologists and assist in removing other misconceptions which may exist.

The present work demonstrates that historical sociological studies which focus on the United States should be of more than an antiquarian interest. This analysis supplies empirical verification for Randall Collins's statement that the early American sociologists were, in many instances, involved with advancing ideology rather than explanation.[22] In this sense, to accept the most popular of the theories of the early sociologists on a prima facie basis is to accept distortions regarding the structure and dynamics of American society. This is evident today in that most contemporary theorists still maintain that the absence of socialism or a radical labor movement in the United States may be traced to the unique or distinctive condition of American society.[23]

It has been said that classical sociology developed as part of a continuing debate with the ghost of Marx. Contemporary American sociology can give rise to a tradition of equal value should it systematically engage the spectre of Commons and the Wisconsin School.

Appendix:
Resolution 52 of the
1893 AFL Convention _____

Whereas, the trade unionists of Great Britain have by the light of experience and the logic of progress, adapted the principle of independent labor politics as an auxiliary to their economic action, and

Whereas such action has resulted in the most gratifying success, and

Whereas, such independent labor politics are based upon the following program, to wit:

1. Compulsory education

2. Direct legislation

3. A legal eight-hour workday

4. Sanitary inspection of workshop, mine and home

5. Liability of employers for injury to health, body, or life

6. The abolition of the contract system in all public work

7. The abolition of the sweating system

8. The municipal ownership of street cars, and gas and electric

9. The nationalization of telegraphs, telephones, railroads and mines

10. The collective ownership by the people of all means of production and distribution

11. The principle of referendum in all legislation. Therefore, Resolved, that this convention hereby indorse the political action of our British comrades, and Resolved that this program and basis of a political labor movement be and is hereby submitted for the favorable consideration of the labor organizations of America, with the request that their delegates to the next annual convention of the American Federation of Labor, be instructed on this most important subject.

Source: American Federation of Labor Convention Proceedings, 1893, pp. 35-37.

_____ Notes _____

1. Introduction

1. In actuality, a number of writers have considered the ideas of early American sociologists. However, most of the works have been written in a descriptive fashion and concentrated on a relatively few sociologists: Ward, Ross, Giddings, Small, Sumner, and Cooley. See: Barnes, *An Introduction to the History of Sociology* (Chicago, 1948); Odum, *American Sociology* (New York, 1951); Beal, *The Development of Sociology in the United States* (Ann Arbor, 1944); Page, *Class and American Sociology* (New York, 1969); and Roscoe and Gisela Hinkle, *The Development of Modern Sociology* (New York, 1968). More recent works are those by Friedrichs, *A Sociology of Sociology* (New York, 1970) and Herman and Julia Schwendinger, *The Sociologists of the Chair* (New York, 1974).

2. Dusky Lee Smith, "Sociology and the Rise of Corporate Capitalism," in Larry Reynolds and Janice Reynolds, *The Sociology of Sociology* (New York, 1970), p. 81.

3. C. Wright Mills, *The Sociological Imagination* (New York, 1959), p. 81.

4. Schwendinger and Schwendinger, op. cit., p. xix.

5. Mark Perlman, *Labor Union Theories in America* (Evanston, Ill., 1958), p. 15.

6. Ibid., p. 4

7. J. H. Abraham, *The Origins and Growth of Sociology* (London, 1973), p. 374.

8. Charles Page, op. cit., pp. 6-7.

9. As Mills noted, much sociology was motivated by an unacknowledged debate with the work of Marx and the challenge of socialist movements. See Mills, op. cit., pp. 81-82. The same observation is made by Zeitlin in reference to European sociology. See Irving Zeitlin, *Ideology*

and the Development of Sociological Theory (Englewood Cliffs, 1968).

10. Page, op. cit., pp. 20 and 113.

11. Benjamin Rader, *The Academic Mind and Reform* (Lexington, Ky., 1966), p. 28.

12. Smith, op. cit.

13. Page, op. cit., p. 21.

14. Ibid.

15. See John Commons, *Myself* (Madison, Wisc., 1934), p. 31.

16. Rader, op. cit., pp. 20-21

17. Staughton Lynd, *American Labor Radicalism* (New York, 1973), p. 17.

18. What is most subject to criticism is Commons's reliance upon two assumptions: the validity of the Turner frontier thesis and the workingmen's acceptance of an ideology of voluntarism. For an understanding of the questionable nature of these assumptions see: Richard Hofstadter, "Turner and the Frontier Myth," *American Scholar* 18, no. 4 (Autumn 1949) and Gary Fink, "The Rejection of Voluntarism," *Industrial and Labor Relations Review* 26, no. 2 (January 1973).

19. According to the Schwendingers, the development of early American sociology occurred between 1883 and 1922. The development of early labor theory occurred during the same era. Ely wrote the first treatise on labor in 1886. Commons's theory was institutionalized in the universities in the early 1920s.

20. "Common sense" is used here in the Gramscian sense of the term. It refers to an uncritical, primarily unconscious, way of viewing social life. It represents the ordinary or taken-for-granted manner of perceiving things during any particular historical era. See Antonio Gramsci, *Selections From the Prison Notebooks* (New York, 1973), especially pp. 417-25.

21. The concept of affinity is employed here with a connotation similar to that provided by Weber for the term "elective affinity." For a description of the Weberian usage see Gerth and Mills, *From Max Weber: Essays in Sociology* (New York, 1970), pp. 62-63. The point in Weber that I wish to emphasize is that unless ideas gain an affinity with the interest of members of special social groups, they die out in the course of history.

22. By "traditional middle class" I refer to small-scale independent businessmen and farmers, and locally based professionals (clergy, teachers, lawyers). The world view of the traditional middle class in sociopolitical terms pictured society as a balance of classes with its pivot and stabilizer in a strong and economically independent middle class. See Mills, *The Power Elite* (New York, 1956), pp. 259-60.

23. For a consideration of the confusion that has arisen over the meaning of Commons's work, see David Seckler's "The Naivete of John R. Commons," *Western Economic Journal* (Summer 1966) and his *Thorstein Veblen and the Institutionalists* (Boulder, Colo., 1975). On the debate over the conservative or liberal nature of Commons's work see W. F. Kennedy, "John R. Commons, Conservative Reformer," *Western Economic Journal* (Fall 1962) and Lafayette Harter, "John R. Commons: Conservative or Liberal," *Western Economic Journal* (Summer 1963).

24. On this see the autobiographies of Ely and Commons: *Ground Under Our Feet* and *Myself*. Also see Dorfman on Henry Carter Adams. It is worthy of note that Ely's concept of "vested interest" bore a great deal of similarity to Commons's notion of "the job-right." On this see Ely's *Property and Contract*, vol. 2. Both conceptions were probably derived from Adams's earlier consideration of the workers' "proprietary right in industry."

2. The Old Economics: Political Economy Prior to 1885

1. Sidney Fine, *Laissez Faire and the General Welfare State* (Ann Arbor, Mich., 1956), p. 47.

2. Richard Hofstadter, *Social Darwinism in American Thought* (Boston, 1955), p. 143.

3. Fine, op. cit., p. 10.

4. Joseph Dorfman, *The Economic Mind in American Civilization* (New York, 1949), p. 49.

5. Ibid., p. 80.

6. Philip Foner, *History of the Labor Movement in the United States*, vol. 1 (New York, 1972), pp. 103-5.

7. Fine, op. cit., pp. 7-10.

8. Edward Kirkland, *Economic History of the United States*, vol. 6 (New York, 1947), pp. 1-2.

9. Harold Faulkner, *Economic History of the United States*, vol. 7 (New York, 1962), p. 9.

10. William Tudor, *Letters on the Eastern States* (Boston, 1821), quoted in Felix Fluget and Harold Faulkner, *Readings in the Economic and Social History of the United States* (New York, 1929), p. 223.

11. V. S. Clark, *History of Manufactures in the United States*, vol. 1 (New York, 1929), p. 455.

12. Norman Ware, *The Industrial Worker, 1840-1860* (Chicago, 1964), p. 51.

13. Fine, op. cit., p. 16.

14. Clark, op. cit., p. 390.

15. Fluget and Faulkner, op. cit., p. 223.

16. Dorfman, op. cit., p. 80.

17. Karl Marx, *Grundrisse* (New York, 1973), p. 884.

18. Fine, op. cit., pp. 16-17.

19. Philip Newman, *The Development of Economic Thought* (Englewood Cliffs, 1952). The so-called nationalist economics represented an early reaction to the English advocacy of free trade. It originated with the German Frederick List, who exerted some influence in America when he toured the nation in the 1830s. Thus, Germanic influence was not completely lacking in American political economy prior to the rise of "the new economics."

20. Henry Carey, *The Harmony of Interests* (Philadelphia, 1890), pp. 215-17.

21. Marx, op. cit., pp. 886-87.

22. William A. Williams, *The Contours of American History* (New York, 1961).

23. Harold Williamson, ed., *The Growth of the American Economy*. (New York, 1951).

24. Jeremy Brecher, *Strike!* (San Francisco, 1972) p. xii.

25. Williamson, op. cit.

26. George Evans, *Business Incorporations in the United States, 1800-1943* (New York, 1948), p. 10.

27. Ibid.

28. Kirkland, op. cit., pp. 199-200.

3. The New Economics: Political Economy after 1885

1. Edward Kirkland, *Economic History of the United States*, vol. 6 (New York, 1947), pp. 212-13. According to Philip Foner, Saint Louis was a city in which workers most closely approached control of the entire municipality. See Foner, *The Great Labor Uprising of 1877* (New York, 1977), pp. 157-87.

2. Official Report of the National Commission on the Causes and Prevention of Violence, Hugh Graham and Ted Gurr, *Violence in America* (New York, 1969), p. 270.

3. Louis Adamic, *Dynamite* (New York, 1931), p. 36.

4. Norman Ware, *Labor Movement in the United States, 1860-1895* (New York, 1929), pp. 48-49.

5. Philip Foner, *History of the Labor Movement in the United States*, vol. 1 (New York, 1972), p. 439.

6. Joseph Dorfman, *The Economic Mind in American Civilization* (New York, 1949), pp. 100-104.

7. Ibid.

8. Ibid.

9. C. Wright Mills, *Sociology and Pragmatism* (New York, 1966), pp. 35-42.

10. Sidney Fine, *Laissez Faire and the General Welfare State* (Ann Arbor, Mich., 1956), p. 11.

11. Dorfman, op. cit., p. 160.

12. Joseph Dorfman, ed., *Two Essays by Henry Carter Adams* (New York, 1969), p. ix.

13. Dorfman, *The Economic Mind*, op. cit., p. 165.

14. Benjamin Rader, *The Academic Mind and Reform* (Lexington, Ky., 1966), p. 13.

15. Mark Perlman, *Labor Union Theories in America* (Evanston, Ill., 1958).

16. Fine, op. cit., p. 52.

17. Philip Newman, *The Development of Economic Thought* (Englewood Cliffs, 1952), p. 186.

18. For an interesting appraisal of Peirce's ideas and their relationship to their social context see C. Wright Mills, *Sociology and Pragmatism* (New York, 1966), chapter 6. For an equally interesting consideration of Lester Ward along similar lines, see Sidney Fine, *Laissez Faire and the General Welfare State* (Ann Arbor, Mich., 1956).

19. Dorfman, *Two Essays*, op. cit., pp. 150-151.

20. For a good account of this period of labor history see Louis Adamic, *Dynamite* (New York, 1931), especially pp. 21-50.

21. Dorfman, op. cit., pp. 41-46.

22. Adamic, op. cit., pp. 41-46.

23. Ware, op. cit., p. 66.

24. William Dick, *Labor and Socialism in America* (Port Washington, N. Y., 1972), see especially chapter 2.

25. Quoted in Foner, op. cit., p. 177.

26. Robert Wiebe, *The Search for Order* (New York, 1967).

27. Ibid.

4. Richard T. Ely and the Search for a New Morality

1. Mark Perlman, *Labor Union Theories in America* (Evanston, Ill., 1958), p. 21.

2. See Ely's *The Labor Movement in America* (New York, 1886), and Rader's *The Academic Mind and Reform*, p. 68.

3. Rader, op. cit., p. 75.

4. Ibid., p. 9.

5. Ibid., p. 11.

6. Ibid.

7. Perlman, op. cit., pp. 24-25.

8. Ibid. Ely was certain that business interests had instigated the affair and that he escaped dismissal only because those interests could not exert total influence within a state university. Ely's explanation is discounted by Walter Metzger; see Hofstadter and Metzger, *The Development of Academic Freedom in the United States* (New York, 1955), pp. 442-33.

9. Ibid., p. 25.

10. Rader, op. cit., p. 16.

11. Richard Ely, *Forum* 18 (October 1894), quoted in Rader, op. cit., p. 183.

12. Rader, op. cit., p. 29.

13. Ibid., p. 12.

14. Ibid., p. 22.

15. Richard Ely, *Introductions to Political Economy* (New York, 1889), pp. 67-68.

16. See John Commons, *Myself* (Madison, Wisc., 1963), p. 31.

17. Richard Ely, *Ground Under Our Feet: An Autobiography* (New York, 1938), p. 136.

18. Rader, op. cit., p. 60. Also see C. Howard Hopkins, *The Rise of the Social Gospel in American Protestantism* (New Haven, 1967).

19. G.W.F. Hegel, *The Philosophy of History* (New York, 1956), pp. 341 and 451.

20. Richard Ely, *The Labor Movement in America* (New York, 1886), pp. 107-8.

21. Mark Perlman, op. cit., p. 18.

22. C. Wright Mills, *The Power Elite* (New York, 1956), p. 271.

23. Philip Foner, *History of the Labor Movement in the United States*, vol. 2 (New York, 1972), p. 14.

24. V. S. Clark, *History of Manufactures in the United States*, vol. 2 (New York, 1919), p. 174.

25. Edward Kirkland, *Economic History of the United States*, vol. 6 (New York, 1962), p. 210.

26. Foner, op. cit., p. 13.

27. Kirkland, op. cit., p. 73.

28. Jeremy Brecher, *Strike!* (San Francisco, 1972).

29. Foner, op. cit., vol. 1, p. 498.

30. Foner, op. cit., vol. 2, p. 171.

31. Ely, *The Labor Movement*, op. cit., pp. 107-8.

32. Ely, *Introduction to Political Economy*, op. cit., p. 69.

33. Ibid., p. 26.

34. Rader, op. cit., p. 69

35. Richard Ely, *Outlines of Economics* (New York, 1893), p. 57.

36. Ely, *The Labor Movement*, op. cit.

37. Norman Ware, *Labor Movement in the United States, 1860-1895* (New York, 1929), p. xviii.

38. Foner, op. cit., vol. 1, pp. 433-34.

39. John Commons, *Documentary History of American Industrial Society*, vol. 9 (Glendale, Calif., 1910), pp. 19-24.

40. Selig Perlman, *A History of Trade Unionism in the United States* (New York, 1950), p. 72.

41. Foner, op. cit., vol. 1, p. 507.

42. Ibid., pp. 506-10.

43. Ware, op. cit., p. 66.

44. William Dick, *Labor and Socialism in America* (Port Washington, N.Y., 1972), p. 22.

45. Ware, op. cit., p. 139.

46. Ibid., pp. 150-51.

47. Gerald Grob, *Workers and Utopia* (Evanston, Ill., 1961), p. 51.

48. Foner, op. cit., vol. 2, pp. 158-59.

49. John Commons and associates, *History of Labour in the United States*, vol. 2 (New York, 1918), p. 482.

50. Robert Hoxie, *Trade Unionism in the United States* (New York, 1924), pp. 94-95.

51. Rader, op. cit., p. 10.

52. Ibid., p. 67.

53. Ibid.

54. C. W. Mills, op. cit., p. 259.

55. Ely, *Outlines of Economics*, op. cit., pp. 193-95.

56. Rader, op. cit., p. 132.

57. Ely in *Forum*, quoted in ibid., p. 174.

58. Rader, op. cit., p. 88.

59. Richard Ely, *Property and Contract in their Relation to the Distribution of Wealth*, vol. 2 (New York, 1914), p. 755.

60. Richard Ely, *Socialism: An Examination of its Nature, its Strength and its Weaknesses with Suggestions for Social Reform* (New York, 1894), see pp. 150 and ff.

61. Rader, op. cit., p. 88.

62. Ely, *Outlines of Economics*, op. cit., pp. 262-63.

63. This compatibility was never complete. Though the Schwendingers report that Ely emerged from the 1894 hearing "smelling like a rose," it is true that Ely, himself, believed that big business interests were behind the hearing. John Commons echoed Ely's views on this matter; see the

Schwendingers' *The Sociologists of the Chair* (New York, 1974), pp. 499-500. Also see Hofstadter and Metzger, op. cit.

5. The Social Situation Confronting Henry Carter Adams

1. Mark Perlman, *Labor Union Theories in America* (Evanston, Ill., 1958), p. 164.

2. John Garrity and J. Sternstein, *Encyclopedia of American Biography* (New York, 1964), p. 10.

3. Perlman, op. cit., p. 164.

4. In contrast to the Ely case at Wisconsin, the evidence relating to Adams's dismissal from Cornell is clear. Henry Adams was dismissed upon the complaint of a wealthy benefactor of that university after he heard Adams deliver an unequivocal prolabor speech. Adams accepted his fate without complaint (see Hofstadter and Metzger, *The Development of Academic Freedom in the United States*, New York, 1955, pp. 418-19.) To my knowledge, Adams's university-based research on labor was never funded by sympathetic businessmen.

5. Garraty and Sternstein, op. cit., pp. 10-11.

6. Sidney Fine, *Laissez Faire and the General Welfare State* (Ann Arbor, Mich., 1956), p. 218.

7. Benjamin Rader, *The Academic Mind and Reform* (Lexington, Ky., 1966), p. 37.

8. Ibid., pp. 36-40.

9. Adams denounced the effect that Ely's views produced as a vicious circle. See "Economics and Jurisprudence," in Dorfman, *Two Essays* by Henry Carter Adams (New York, 1969), p. 152.

10. James Weinstein, *The Decline of Socialism in America* (New York, 1967), pp. 45-53.

11. John Laslett, *Labor and the Left* (New York, 1970), p. 6.

12. William Dick, *Labor and Socialism in America* (Port Washington, N.Y., 1972), p. 20.

13. Samuel Gompers, *Seventy Years of Life and Labor*, vol. 1 (New York, 1925), pp. 388-89.

14. Friedrich Engels quoted in Karl Marx and Friedrich Engels, *Letters to Americans* (New York, 1969), p. 305. This should not be taken to imply that Engels necessarily viewed Gompers as a socialist spokesman. Indeed, much criticism was directed at Gompers for his organizing efforts while they remained focused upon the skilled segment of the working class.

15. John Commons and associates, *History of Labour in the United States*, vol. 2 (New York, 1918), p. 305.

16. Ibid., p. 374.

17. Dick, op. cit., p. 18.

18. Ibid., p. 25.

19. Ibid., pp. 47-48.

20. AFL convention proceedings, 1892, p. 12, quoted in Commons, op. cit., p. 500.

21. Gompers to Delahaye, 1891, quoted in Philip Foner, *History of the Labor Movement in the United States*, vol. 2 (New York, 1972), p. 177.

22. Ibid., p. 183.

23. Samuel Gompers, *New York Herald Tribune* (Jan. 7, 1894), quoted in ibid., p. 311.

24. Ibid., pp. 203-18.

25. Herbert Miller, "Socialism in the United States," *American Federationist* 2 (August 1895): 97, quoted in ibid., p. 279.

26. V. S. Clark, *History of Manufactures in the United States*, vol. 3 (New York, 1929), p. 5.

27. Harold Faulkner, *The Economic History of the United States*, vol. 7 (New York, 1962), p. 453.

28. Felix Flugel and Harold Faulkner, *Readings in the Economic and Social History of the United States* (New York, 1929), pp. 504-9.

29. Irwin Yellowitz, *The Position of the Worker in American Society, 1865-96.*

30. Alain Touraine, *Workers' Attitudes to Technical Change* (Organization for Economic Co-operation and Development, 1965), p. 20. Also see David Montgomery's *Workers' Control in America* (New York, 1979). I am in great debt to Montgomery's overall approach for my consideration of the autonomy issue.

31. For a discussion of worker autonomy and its relationship to alienation see: William Faunce, *Problems of Industrial Society* (New York, 1968), and Robert Blauner, *Alienation and Freedom* (Chicago, 1964). Though each of these authors provides a good and concise consideration of the issue, neither of them grasps the problem in its fullest complexity.

32. For an updated consideration of this process see Harry Braverman, *Labor and Monopoly Capital* (New York, 1974).

33. Arthur Kornhauser, Robert Dubin, and Arthur Ross, *Industrial Conflict* (New York, 1954), pp. 214-15.

34. Ibid.

35. Harry Jerome, *Mechanization in Industry* (New York, 1934), pp. 350-51. There has been a long-term interest in investigating the vagaries of the business cycle beginning with Wesley Mitchell's *Business Cycles* (New York, 1927). For more recent studies relevant to the point under discussion see: Edwin Frickey, *Economic Fluctuations in the United States,*

1866-1914 (New York, 1942); Joseph Schumpeter, *Business Cycles: A Theoretical, Historical and Statistical Analysis of the Capitalist Process*, 2 vols. (New York, 1939); Arthur F. Burns, *The Business Cycle in a Changing World* (New York, 1969).

36. Theodore Levitt, "Prosperity Versus Strikes," *Industrial and Labor Relations Review* 6, no. 2 (January 1953): 220-26.

37. Jack Skeels, "Measures of U.S. Strike Activity," *Industrial and Labor Relations Review* 24, no. 4 (July 1971): 523. Since Hansen's early study, economistic explanations for trade union behavior have been prevalent. In addition to the work of Skeels and Hansen see: Florence Peterson, "Strikes in the United States, 1880-1936," Department of Labor, Bureau of Labor Statistics, bulletin 651 (1937); Orley Ashenfelter and George Johnson, "Bargaining Theory, Trade Unions and Industrial Strike Activity," *American Economic Review* 59 (1969); D. Britt and O. Galle, "Structural Antecedents of the Shape of Strikes: A Comparative Analysis," *American Sociological Review* 39 (October 1974); R. N. Stern, "Intermetropolitan Patterns of Strike Frequency," *Industrial and Labor Relations Review* 29 (January 1976). For a good summary of recent work and thinking on interpreting strike behavior, see chapter 5 in Ivar Berg, *Industrial Sociology* (Englewood Cliffs, 1979). A fuller consideration is afforded in Ivar Berg, Freedman, and Freeman, *Managers and Work Reform* (New York, 1978).

38. Dale Yoder, "Economic Changes and Industrial Unrest in the United States," *Journal of Political Economy* 48 (1940): 234.

39. Reinhard Bendix, *Work and Authority in Industry* (Berkeley, Calif., 1974), pp. 254-55.

40. See David Montgomery, "The 'New Unionism' and the Transformation of Workers' Consciousness in America, 1909-1922," *Journal of Social History* (Summer 1974).

41. Richard Edwards, *Contested Terrain* (New York, 1979), p. 51.

42. David Snyder, "Institutional Setting and Industrial Conflict: Comparative Analyses of France, Italy, and the United States," *American Sociological Review* 40 (June 1975): 265.

43. Ibid.

44. Ibid.

45. Commons, op. cit., vol. 2, pp. 358-59.

46. Joseph Schumpeter, *History of Economic Analysis* (New York, 1961), p. 83.

47. V. S. Clark, op. cit., vol. 2, p. 170.

48. Commons, op. cit., pp. 509-10.

49. Ibid., p. 511.

50. John Hobson, *The Evolution of Modern Capitalism* (New York, 1926), p. 278.

51. George Barnett, *Chapters on Machinery and Labor* (Cambridge, Mass., 1926), p. 278.

52. John Laslett, op. cit., p. 168.

53. Ibid., p. 16.

54. Ibid., p. 16.

55. Ibid., pp. 109-10.

56. Foner, op. cit., vol. 2, pp. 215-16.

57. Ibid., p. 399.

58. The 1893 AFL convention was perhaps the only convention wherein socialist political programs were open to consideration by all assembled delegates. As directed by the convention, the socialist political proposal was to be put before all delegates for deliberation, and a final vote was to be conducted during the 1894 proceedings. However, after protracted argument and bureaucratic maneuverings, the essence of the socialist proposal was desiccated and the form of the proposal which finally emerged was tabled. It was at the 1893 meeting that Gompers was defeated for the presidency of the AFL by John McBride. It may have been that delegates were punishing Gompers and the Federation's bureaucracy for thwarting what was perceived of as the will of the convention. (See pp. 38-43 of the 1893 AFL proceedings.)

After 1894 socialist-inspired resolutions were virtually always blocked within committees and never considered before a plenary meeting of the delegates. (See AFL convention proceedings, 1899-1908 and 1912-1917.)

59. Of course, the procedures undertaken here afford, by necessity, only an indirect test of the relationship between the autonomy issue and socialistic sympathies. Unionists may have voted to remove the "for favorable consideration" phraseology for reasons other than the presence of the autonomy issue (e.g., ideological principle, reaction to bureaucratic maneuverings, friendships, personal loyalties, etc.). Given the great possibility of interference by extraneous factors such as those described above, the intensity of the measures of association which were obtained probably tend to be rather understated.

60. Not included in the data for Tables 4 and 5 were the votes of mixed and not distinctly trades-union affiliates such as federal labor unions, central labor unions, state branches, and trades councils. Also excluded were trades unions for which no estimate was possible with regard to the presence or absence of the autonomy issue. Excluded for this latter reason were the Typographia (German-American), the Hotel and Restaurant Workers, and the Horseshoers (all voting "favorable"). Also excluded were the Tanners and Curriers, Theatrical State Employees, Piano Tuners, and the Tobacco Pressmen's Helpers (all voting

"not favorable"). By virtue of the above exclusions approximately 10 percent of the pure trades-unionist votes was not included in the data.

61. Montgomery, op. cit.

62. Foster Dulles, *Labor in America* (New York, 1966), p. 185.

63. Barnett, op. cit., pp. 140-42.

64. Foner, op. cit., vol. 3, p. 62.

65. Faulkner, op. cit., p. 453.

66. Selig Perlman, *A History of Trade Unionism in the United States* (New York, 1950), p. 196.

67. Foner, op. cit., p. 69.

68. Leo Wolman, *The Growth of American Trade Unionism, 1880-1923*

69. Faulkner, op. cit., p. 290.

70. Commons, op. cit., vol. 2, p. 524.

71. Faulkner, op. cit., p. 301.

72. Commons, op. cit., vol. 2, p. 532.

73. Faulkner, op. cit., p. 292.

6. Henry Carter Adams Addresses the Labor Problem

1. Quoted in Joseph Dorfman, *Two Essays by Henry Carter Adams* (New York: 1969), p. 8.

2. Henry Carter Adams, "Relation of the State to Industrial Action," *Publications of the American Economics Association* 1 (January 1887): 544. A number of Adams's essays are available through a more accessible source: see Joseph Dorfman, *Two Essays by Henry Carter Adams* (New York, 1969). For the relevant passage here, consult Dorfman, p. 129.

3. Ibid., p. 490. See Dorfman, pp. 67-68.

4. Ibid., p. 512. See Dorfman, p. 99.

5. Henry Carter Adams, "An Interpretation of the Social Movements of Our Time," *International Journal of Ethics* 2 (October 1891): 45. See Dorfman, p. 199.

6. Adams, "Relation of the State to Industrial Action," op. cit., pp. 487-88. See Dorfman, pp. 63-67.

7. Ibid., pp. 494 and 541-42. See Dorfman, pp. 99 and 127.

8. Ibid., p. 546. See Dorfman, p. 133.

9. Mark Perlman, *Labor Union Theories in America* (Evanston, Ill., 1958), p. 167.

10. Adams, "Relation of the State to Industrial Action," op. cit., pp. 494-95.

11. See G.D.H. Cole, *A Short History of the English Working Class* (London, 1965). As Cole documented, the wave of unionization which swept England in the late nineteenth century provided a major impetus to the development of a socialistically oriented trade unionism.

12. Dorfman, op. cit., pp. 33-35.

13. Henry Carter Adams, "An Interpretation of the Social Movements of Our Time," op. cit., pp. 40-41. See Dorfman, pp. 193-95.

14. Henry Carter Adams, "Economics and Jurisprudence." *Economic Studies* 2 (February, 1897): 24-33. See Dorfman, pp. 152-60.

15. Harry Braverman, *Labor and Monopoly Capital* (New York, 1964).

16. Adams, "Relation of the State to Industrial Action," op. cit., p. 544. See Dorfman, p. 99.

17. Ibid., p. 512. See Dorfman, p. 129.

18. Adams, "Economics and Jurisprudence," op. cit., p. 35. See Dorfman, p. 162.

19. Adams, "An Interpretation of the Social Movements of Our Time," op. cit., p. 32. See Dorfman, p. 186.

20. Adams, "Economics and Jurisprudence," op. cit., p. 13. See Dorfman, p. 154.

21. Adams, "An Interpretation of the Social Movements of Our Time," op. cit., p. 520. See Dorfman, pp. 106-7.

22. Ibid.

23. Ibid., p. 546. See Dorfman, p. 130.

24. Adams, "Economics and Jurisprudence," op. cit., pp. 24-33. See Dorfman, pp. 152-60.

25. Dorfman, op. cit., pp. 38-39.

7. John Commons and the Pre-Wisconsin Years

1. John Commons, *Myself* (Madison, Wisc., 1963), p. 143.

2. Ibid., p. 8.

3. Ibid.

4. Ibid., p. 26.

5. Ibid., p. 42.

6. Ibid., pp. 44-45.

7. Ibid., p. 53.

8. Ibid., p. 54.

9. Ibid., p. 47.

10. Ibid., p. 67.

11. American Academy of Political and Social Science, *Social Legislation and Social Activity* (Philadelphia, 1902), pp. 25-26.

12. Commons, op. cit., pp. 170-71.

13. Ibid., p. 87.

14. Ibid., p. 88.

15. John Commons, *Legal Foundations of Capitalism* (Madison, Wisc., 1968), p. 376.

16. See Commons, *Myself*, op. cit., pp. 96-97, and his *Institutional*

Economics (New York, 1934), p. 617.

17. Joseph Dorfman, *The Economic Mind in American Civilization* (New York, 1949), p. 293.

18. Commons, *Myself*, op. cit., p. 133.

19. Ibid., p. 135. Aside from Macy, Vanderbilt, and Carnegie, Commons's work was financed by Robert Hunter, a wealthy New Yorker, and Stanley McCormick, a Chicago businessman. These two men each donated $10,000. See Benjamin Rader, *The Academic Mind and Reform* (Lexington, Ky., 1966), p. 167.

20. Ibid., p. 137.

21. Ibid., pp. 139-40.

8. John Commons and the Wisconsin School in Full Bloom

1. John Commons, *Documentary History of American Industrial Society* (Glendale, Calif., 1910), vol. 3, p. 93.

2. John Commons and associates, *History of Labour in the United States*, vol. 1 (New York, 1918), p. 26.

3. Ibid., p. 3.

4. Selig Perlman, *A Theory of the Labor Movement* (New York, 1949) p. 208.

5. Commons, *History*, op. cit., p. 17.

6. Ibid., pp. 4-9.

7. See Philip Foner, *History of the Labor Movement in the United States*, vol. 1 (New York, 1972), p. 11.

8. Commons, *Myself*, (Madison, Wisc., 1963), p. 190.

9. Commons, *History*, op. cit., pp. 5-11.

10. Ibid., vol. 2, p. 472.

11. John Commons, *Institutional Economics* (New York, 1934), p. 766.

12. Ibid., pp. 769-73.

13. Commons, *History*, vol. 2, op. cit., p. 525.

14. Ibid., p. 527.

15. Harold Faulkner, *The Economic History of the United States*, vol. 7 (New York, 1962), p. 289.

16. Selig Perlman and Philip Taft, *History of Labor in the United States, 1896-1932* (New York, 1935), p. 49.

17. Commons, *History*, vol. 1, op. cit., pp. 617-18.

18. Selig Perlman, *A History of Trade Unionism in the United States* (New York, 1950), p. 167.

19. Ibid., p. 489.

20. Leo Wolman, *Ebb and Flow in Trade Unionism* (New York, 1936), p. 16.

21. Perlman and Taft, op. cit., pp. 13-15.

22. Ibid., pp. 49-50.

23. Thomas Brooks, *Toil and Trouble* (New York, 1964), pp. 109-10.

24. Faulkner, op. cit., p. 309.

25. Ibid.

26. Ibid., pp. 310-14.

27. Graham Adams, *Age of Industrial Violence, 1910-15* (New York, 1966), p. xii.

28. Ibid., p. 215.

29. Ibid., pp. 216-17.

30. See Adams in Dorfman, *Two Essays by Henry Carter Adams* (New York, 1969), p. 129.

31. Marc Karson, *American Labor Unions and Politics, 1900-1918* (Carbondale, Ill., 1958), p. 99.

32. Gary Fink, "The Rejection of Voluntarism," *Industrial and Labor Relations Review* 26, no. 2 (January 1973): 805.

33. From *The Nation* (October 1919) quoted in Jeremy Brecher, *Strike!* (San Francisco, 1972), p. 101.

34. Ibid., p. 103.

35. V. S. Clark, *History of Manufactures in the United States*, vol. 3 (New York, 1929), p. 299.

36. George Soule, *The Economic History of the United States*, vol. 9 (New York, 1947), pp. 59-61.

37. Brecher, op. cit., p. 128.

38. Clark, op. cit., p. 304.

39. Foner, op. cit., p. 11. The notion that his theory completely justified the practices of the AFL bureaucracy did not originate with Commons. Rather, Samuel Gompers claimed Commons's work as a justification for his own approach to the organization of American workers. Gompers offered such an opinion soon after the original publication of Commons's history (Philip Foner to DeBrizzi, August 1978). This is a significant point in the consideration of Commons's alleged role as an apologist.

40. John Commons, *Races and Immigrants in America* (New York, 1907), p. 5.

41. Ibid., p. 12.

42. Ibid., p. 20.

43. Ibid., pp. 153-55.

44. Ibid., p. 169.

45. Commons may have been inspired on this point by his colleague at Wisconsin, Grover Huebner. In a 1906 article, "The Americanization of the Immigrant," Huebner wrote, "trade unionism is the greatest Americanization force for the adult immigrants in the cities and large industrial cen-

ters." Among other things, union membership among immigrants was said to teach self-government, a sense of public purpose, sense of American identity, and American customs and ideals: "In other words, it enables him, the immigrant, to adopt the American social and moral standard of living." See Huebner, *Annals of the American Academy of Political and Social Science* 27 (May 1906): 653-75.

46. See Commons's *Myself* and *Legal Foundations of Capitalism*, op. cit.

47. Mark Perlman, *Labor Union Theories in America* (Evanston, Ill., 1958), p. 171.

48. Ibid., pp. 172-73.

49. See William Williams, *The Contours of American History* (New York, 1961), especially "The Age of Corporate Capitalism, 1882-" and ff.

50. Before World War I the legitimacy of capitalism in America was seriously being questioned, due to the conditions considered here. Yet, as Elwin Powell has cogently argued, "By 1919 the business class was in clear if insecure ascendancy . . . its new position of dominance had yet to be ratified by public consensus. . . . The essence of the new consensus was Americanism, which was manufactured during the war and extended to legitimize the corporate order." (See Powell, *The Design of Discord* [New York, 1970], pp. 100-103.)

Apparently, the new order was legitimated. In the 1920s big business had its interests catered to in a big way. Tariffs were raised, tax benefits for the rich were instituted, and business consolidation was encouraged. In fact, the Federal Trade Commission, originally brought about by progressives to check the expansion of big business, was the primary means by which corporated consolidation was advanced. See Richard Hofstadter, *The Age of Reform* (New York, 1955), p. 285.

51. Murray Levin, *Political Hysteria in America*, pp. 113-15. Also see Robert Wiebe, *The Search for Order* (New York, 1967), p. 290.

52. According to Powell "Americanism" connoted the belief that no fault could be attributed to American institutions. The origin of social problems could be traced, ultimately, to faulty individuals (Powell, op. cit., p. 103).

53. Commons's thesis of American exceptionalism dovetailed nicely with the new emphasis on Americanist ideology. None of the other theorists considered in this study has included such views as an integral component within their labor theories. As Hofstadter observed: "Hostility to immigrants was probably most common near the extreme ends of the political spectrum among those Progressives whose views were most influenced by the Populist inheritance." Hofstadter specifically refers to Commons on this point. (See Hofstadter, op. cit., pp. 178-79.)

54. Philip G. Wright, "Contest in Congress Between Organized Labor and Business," in *Quarterly Journal of Economics* 29 (February 1915): 238.

55. At U.S. Steel the welfare measures were instituted after labor disputes during which unions in the corporation's plants were virtually crushed. See John Garraty, "The United States Steel Corporation Versus Labor: The Early Years," in *Labor History* 1 (Winter 1960): 3-38.

56. Charles Gulick, *Labor Policy of the United States Steel Corporation* (New York, 1924), pp. 138-50.

57. Garraty, op. cit., pp. 9-20.

58. George Gibb and Evelyn Knowlton, *The Resurgent Years 1911-1927* (New York, 1956), pp. 138-39.

59. Paul Kellogg, "Pioneering by Employers," in *Survey* 26 (Aug. 19, 1911) 712-717.

60. "Pro-Labor Pleas from Capitalists," in *Literary Digest* 59 (Feb. 6, 1915): 230-31.

61. Ibid., p. 231.

62. Gibb and Knowlton, op. cit., p. 253.

63. Raynall Bolling, "The United States Steel Corporation and Labor," in *American Academy of Political and Social Science* 42: (July 1912) 25-37.

64. Charles Schwab, "Capital and Labor," in *American Academy of Political and Social Science* 81 (January, 1919) 157-62.

65. The single best history of the strike remains David Brody's *Labor in Crisis* (New York, 1965).

66. Gulick, op. cit., p. 94.

67. See the discussions of Gulick and Brody, op. cit.

68. Carleton Parker, "The Labor Policy of the American Trusts, 1914," in *Atlantic Monthly* 125 (February 1920) 225-234.

69. Gibb and Knowlton, op. cit., p. 142.

70. Ronald Prezioso, "The Oil Industry in Bayonne: Its Rise and Decline" (1976), unpublished manuscript, New Jersey Reference Collection, Municipal Library of Bayonne, N.J.

71. F. Van Z. Lane, *Bayonne, New Jersey: Its Location, Industries, Advantages, and History* (Bayonne Chamber of Commerce, 1916), n.p.

72. Prezioso, op. cit., p. 14.

73. Gibb and Knowlton, op. cit., p. 140.

74. Ibid., p. 684.

75. *Survey* 34 (July 31, 1915): 387.

76. The *Jersey Journal* (July 20, 1915), pp. 1 and 4.

77. Otey S. Jones, in collaboration with Tim Ziobro, *A Short History of Bayonne, New Jersey* (1971), p. 131, unpublished manuscript, N.J. Reference Collection, Bayonne, N.J.

78. Gibb and Knowlton, op. cit., pp. 142-47.

79. *New York Call* (July 25, 1915).

80. Cited in ibid.

81. "Bloodshed in Labor Wars," *Literary Digest* 57 (Aug. 7, 1915): 237 and 256.

82. The *Jersey Journal* (July 23, 1915), p. 5.

83. John A. Fitch, "When A Sheriff Breaks a Strike," in *Survey* 34 (July 31, 1915): 415.

84. Ibid.

85. Ibid.

86. Ibid.

87. Ibid.

88. Ibid.

89. Fitch, op. cit., p. 416.

90. Prezioso, op. cit., p. 18.

91. *New York Call* (July 30, 1915), p. 1.

92. Federal Writers' Project of the WPA, *New Jersey—A Guide to the Present and Past* (New York, 1946), p. 204.

93. The *Evening Review* (Oct. 7, 1916).

94. Ibid. (Oct. 9, 1916).

95. Ibid. (Oct. 11 and 12, 1916).

96. "Newspaper Incitement to Violence," *New Republic* 8 (Oct. 21, 1916): 283-85.

97. Ibid.

98. John A. Fitch, "The Explosion at Bayonne," in *Survey* 37 (Oct. 21, 1916): 61-62.

99. Ibid.

100. "The End of the Bayonne Strike," in the *Independent* 88 (Oct. 30, 1916): 186.

101. Ibid.

102. The *Evening Review* (Oct. 20, 1916), p. 4.

103. John D. Rockefeller, Jr., " Labor and Capital—Partners," in *Atlantic Monthly* 117 (January 1916): 19.

104. Gibb and Knowlton, op. cit., p. 151.

105. "Conflicting Labor Policy," in *New Republic* 14 (Feb. 16, 1918): 73-74.

106. Arbitrator, "A Businessman's Reflections on Labor Problems," in *American Journal of Sociology* 21 (January 1916): 456-57. The author wished to remain anonymous. Unfortunately, the author's identity must remain unknown since the early records and correspondences of AJS mistakenly were destroyed a few years ago (Helen Bidwell to DeBrizzi, May 1979).

9. Institutionalization of Commons-Wisconsin Theory

1. Edward Kirkland, *Dream and Thought in the Business Community, 1860-1900* (Ithaca, N.Y., 1956), pp. 2 and 16-17.
2. C. R. Henderson, "Business Men and Social Theorists," in *American Journal of Sociology* 1 (January 1896): 388.
3. Ibid., p. 389.
4. Kirkland, op. cit., p. 84.
5. Philip G. Wright, "Contest in Congress Between Organized Labor and Business," in *Quarterly Journal of Economics* 29 (February, 1915): 244.
6. Frederick Rudolph, *The American College and University: A History* (New York, 1962), p. 425. Also see Clark Spence, *The Sinews of American Capitalism* (New York, 1962), p. 195.
7. Rudolph, op. cit. Also, Allan Nevins, *Study in Power, John D. Rockefeller: Industrialist and Philanthropist*, vol. 2 (New York, 1953), pp. 189-92.
8. Rudolph, op. cit., p. 48.
9. Laurence Veysey, *The Emergence of the American University* (Chicago, 1965), p. 410.
10. Ibid.
11. Rudolph, op. cit., p. 427.
12. Henry S. Pritchett, "Shall the University Become a Business Corporation?" in *Atlantic Monthly* 96 (September 1905): 295.
13. Frederick Jackson Turner to Joseph Schafer (May 22, 1902), quoted in Veysey, op. cit., pp. 388-89.
14. Ibid., p. 411.
15. Quoted in ibid., p. 275.
16. Kirkland, op. cit., p. 88.
17. Ibid., pp. 88-89.
18. Charles Eliot, "Employers' Policies in the Industrial Strike," in *Harper's* 110 (March 1905): 529.
19. Veysey, op. cit., p. 411.
20. For a consideration of the problems that Ely and Adams confronted in the university, see the discussions provided in the earlier chapters of this work. Marxism represented another alternative to the Commons theory, but it had no well-known proponents in the schools. See Mark Perlman, *Labor Union Theories in America* (Evanston, Ill., 1958), pp. 17-20.
21. "Freedom of Speech and Political Issues at Western State Universities," in *Current Opinion* 58 (June 1915): 419-20.
22. Rudolph, op. cit., pp. 434 and ff.

23. Perlman, op. cit., p. 30.

24. Ibid., pp. 25-31 and 37-42.

25. Arthur M. Gordon, "Businessmen and Scholars," in *Nation* 93 (Sept. 14, 1911): 238-39.

26. "Report of the Committee of the American Association of University Professors on Academic Freedom and Academic Tenure," in *School and Society* 3 (Jan. 22, 1916): 109-21.

27. "The Burning Issue of Free Speech at Eastern as well as Western Universities," in *Current Opinion* 59 (August 1915): 111-13.

28. "Collective Bargaining and Colorado," in *Survey* 33 (Jan. 16, 1915): 426.

29. Ibid., p. 427.

30. Andrew Carnegie, "The Future of Labor," in *Annals of the American Academy of Political and Social Science* 33 (March 1909): 239-45.

31. Henry S. Pritchett, "The Policy of the Carnegie Foundation for the Advancement of Teaching," in *Educational Review* 32 (June 1906): 84.

32. Ibid.

33. Joseph Wall, *Andrew Carnegie* (New York, 1970), p. 834.

34. Louis Hacker, *The World of Andrew Carnegie* (New York, 1968), p. 65.

35. Ibid., p. 16.

36. Ibid., pp. 358-62.

37. Ibid., pp. 435-38, and David Brody, *Labor in Crisis* (New York, 1965), p. 15.

38. Nevins, op. cit., pp. 255-68.

39. See chapter 8.

40. Michael Mulkay, *Science and the Sociology of Knowledge* (London, 1979), pp. 96-98.

41. Paul McNulty, *The Origins and Development of Labor Economics* (Cambridge, Mass., 1980), p. 171.

42. John S. Brubacker and Willis Rudy, *Higher Education in Transition*, 3rd ed. (New York, 1976), pp. 167-68.

43. McNulty, op. cit., p. 170.

44. Robert Wiebe, *Business and Reform* (Cambridge, Mass., 1962), p. 212.

45. Levin Schucking, *The Sociology of Literary Taste*, reprinted 1923 (Chicago, 1966), p. 45.

46. James Morris, *Conflict within the AFL: A Study of Craft versus Industrial Unionism, 1901-1938* (Ithaca, N.Y., 1958), p. 38.

47. Harold Livesay, *Samuel Gompers and Organized Labor in America* (Boston, 1978), p. 197.

48. Philip Taft, *The A.F. of L. in the Time of Gompers* (New York, 1957), p. xix.

49. Livesay, op. cit., p. 180.

50. Marguerite Green, *The National Civic Federation and the American Labor Movement, 1900-1925*, reprinted 1956 (Westport, Conn., 1973), p. 389.

51. Robert Murray, *Red Scare: A Study in National Hysteria, 1919-1920*, reprinted 1955 (Westport, Conn., 1980), p. 87.

52. Ibid., pp. 173 and 263.

53. Ibid., p. 1970.

54. Morris, op. cit., p. 93.

55. Ibid., pp. 89-90 and 116.

56. Taft, op. cit., p. 368.

57. Morris, op. cit., p. 70.

58. McNulty, op. cit., p. 162.

59. John Aiken and James McDonnell, "Walter Rausenbusch and Labor Reform: A Social Gospeller's Approach," in *Labor History* 11 (Spring 1970): 133.

60. On some occasions Commons did recognize the logical implications of the close of the western frontier. With the "safety valve" gone, class conflict could be expected to rise. For this reason Commons viewed the advent of the large corporation as a propitious historical occurrence. This was true to the extent that the complex division of labor within the corporation provided a substitute "safety valve" in the form of increased chances for promotion. See Commons, "Is Class Conflict in America Growing and Is It Inevitable?" *Papers and Proceedings of the American Sociological Society* 2 (December 1907): 138-48.

61. In contemporary accounts of labor theory Commons is consistently cited while Ely and Adams are systematically ignored; if considered, they generally are not presented as major theorists. See Milton Derber, *Research in Labor Problems in the United States* (New York, 1967); Mark Perlman, *Labor Union Theories in America* (Evanston, Ill., 1958); Industrial Relations Research Association, *Interpreting the Labor Movement* (Madison, Wisc., 1952).

As should be recalled from the analysis presented earlier, Ely's consideration of the labor movement eventually arrived at conclusions similar to those maintained by the old (laissez-faire) economics proponents. Since Ely called for the overt repression of labor organizations, he could offer no new solutions to the labor problem. In addition, Ely's theory always retained Statist implications.

Though Henry Carter Adams's analysis did provide clear and useful suggestions to defuse the militancy of labor, his analysis shared no affinity with the interests and outlook of big business. This followed from the fact that Adams's theory exposed the structural faults of the American political-economic structure and subjected to question the ideology of the captains of industry. Also, given the tight connection which existed between the theoretical structure of Adams's work and the conclusions which he developed, it was difficult to reinterpret those conclusions in any way other than Adams originally intended them. As demonstrated in chapter 8, the reverse situation was true with regard to the relationship of theoretical structure and conclusions in Commons's work.

62. See David Noble's review of Lafayette Harter's *John R. Commons: His Assault on Laissez-Faire* in *Labor History* 4 (Fall 1963): 290.

10. Conclusion

1. E. P. Thompson, *The Poverty of Theory and Other Essays* (New York, 1975): p. 235.

2. See Commons's autobiography, *Myself* (Madison, Wis., 1936).

3. Robert Wiebe, *The Search for Order* (Madison, Wis., 1967), pp. 294-96.

4. Staughton Lynd, *American Labor Radicalism* (New York, 1973), p. 17.

5. As noted in chapter 8, "Americanism" became a new legitimating ideology for the political economy of the United States circa 1920. That ideology was retained through the New Deal and beyond. However, as Sidney Lens has shown, had President Roosevelt resorted to "union busting" (as was done in the 1920s), the New would have collapsed. See Lens, *The Labor Wars* (Garden City, 1974), p. 287. This was the case in that business interests had withdrawn their support from the president after the inclusion of prolabor clauses in section 7(a) of the National Industrial Recovery Act (NIRA). See Link and Catton, *The American Epoch*, vol. 2 (New York, 1973), pp. 148-49. In short, the ideology of "Americanism" could not be sustained in the same manner as it had been in the 1920s in that the alignment of social classes had changed. Roosevelt became more prolabor out of necessity in that, after the withdrawal of business backing, the State was forced to strike a new vein of support. What is most ironic regarding this matter is that section 7(a) was originally included in the NIRA in order to countenance legally questionable business practices commonly employed by monopolistic industries. See Lens, op. cit., p. 288.

6. Perlman's most famous work was *A Theory of the Labor Movement* (New York, 1949). Taft continued to carry on the Wisconsin tradition during the 1960s. For a sample of Taft's work see his *Organized Labor in American History* (New York, 1964).

7. See the comments of John Dunlop in R. Rowan and H. Northrup, eds., *Readings in Labor Economics and Labor Relations* (Homewood, Ill., 1968), pp. 43-48.

8. Philip Foner, *History of the Labor Movement in the United States*, vol. 1 (New York, 1972), p. 11.

9. See Michael Rogin, "Voluntarism: The Political Function of an Antipolitical Doctrine," in *Industrial and Labor Relations Review* 15 (July 1962): 521-35, and Gary Fink, "The Rejection of Voluntarism," in *Industrial and Labor Relations Review* 26 (January 1973): 805-19.

10. See, for example, the debate between Kennedy and Harter in *The Western Economic Journal* (Summer 1963 and Fall 1962).

11. For a consideration of "balance theory" see C. Wright Mills, *White Collar and the Power Elite*, especially chapter 11.

12. For an excellent discussion of the second thrust and the implications within it see William A. Williams's *The Contours of American History* (New York, 1961). In addition, one must not forget that there was never a total compatibility between the early sociologists and their business patrons. All three of the theorists considered in this study were either challenged or dismissed from university positions for criticisms which they directed at business. For a thorough consideration of the relationship between business and the universities in the early twentieth century, see Metzger, "Academic Freedom and Big Business," pp. 413-67 in Hofstadter and Metzger, *The Development of Academic Freedom in the United States* (New York, 1955).

13. John Commons and John Andrews, *Principles of Labor Legislation* (1916), 4th rev. ed. 1936 (New York, 1967), p. 476.

14. Ibid., p. 479.

15. Ibid., p. 489.

16. Alvin Gouldner, *The Future of the Intellectuals and the Rise of the New Class* (New York, 1979). See the discussion on pp. 16-20.

17. David Seckler, "The Naivete of John R. Commons," in *The Western Economic Journal* (Summer 1966): 261-67.

18. David Seckler, *Thorstein Veblen and the Institutionalists* (Boulder, Colo., 1975), p. 126.

19. See note 1, Chapter 1.

20. Roscoe Hinkle and Gisela Hinkle, *The Development of Modern Sociology* (New York, 1968), pp. 2-4.

21. See Herman Schwendinger and Julia Schwendinger, *The Sociologists of the Chair* (New York, 1974), p. 163; also Dusky Lee Smith, "Sociology and the Rise of Corporate Capitalism," in Larry Reynolds and Janice Reynolds, *The Sociology of Sociology* (New York, 1970).

22. Randall Collins, *Conflict Sociology* (New York, 1975), pp. 531-534

23. Daniel Bell, *Marxian Socialism in the United States* (Princeton, 1967), p. vii. For an example of sociological theory in this genre, see S. M. Lipset, *The First New Nation* (New York, Anchor Books, 1963), especially chapter 5, "Trade Unions and the American Value System."

___ Bibliography _____

Abraham, J. S. *The Origins and Growth of Sociology*. London: Penguin, 1973.
Adamic, Louis. *Dynamite*. New York: Viking Press, 1931.
Adams, Graham. *Age of Industrial Violence, 1910-15*. New York: Columbia University Press, 1966.
Adams, Henry Carter. "Relation of the State to Industrial Action." *Publications of the American Economics Association* 1 (January 1887).
———. "An Interpretation of the Social Movements of Our Time." *International Journal of Ethics* 2 (October 1891).
———. "Economics and Jurisprudence." *Economic Studies* 2 (February 1897).
Aiken, John, and James McDonnell. "Walter Rausenbusch and Labor Reform: A Social Gospeller's Approach." *Labor History* 2 (Spring 1970).
American Academy of Political and Social Science. *Social Legislation and Social Activity*. Philadelphia: 1902.
American Federation of Labor. *History, Encyclopedia and Reference Book* Washington, D.C.: 1919.
———. *Convention Proceedings*. Washington, D.C.: 1893-1908; 1912-1917.
Arbitrator. "A Businessman's Reflections on Labor Problems." *American Journal of Sociology* 21 (January 1916).
Aronowitz, Stanley. *False Promises*. New York: McGraw-Hill, 1973.
Ashenfelter, Orley, and George Johnson. "Bargaining Theory, Trade Unions and Industrial Strike Activity." *American Economic Review* 59 (1969).
Barnes, Harry E., ed. *An Introduction to the History of Sociology*. Chicago: University of Chicago Press, 1948.
Barnett, George. *Chapters on Machinery and Labor*. Cambridge: Harvard University Press, 1926.

Bell, Daniel. *Marxian Socialism in the United States*. Princeton: Princeton University Press, 1967.

Bendix, Reinhard. *Work and Authority in Industry*. Berkeley: University of California Press, 1974.

Berg, Ivar. *Industrial Sociology*. Englewood Cliffs: Prentice-Hall, 1979.

Berg, Ivar; Freedman and Freedman. *Managers and Work Reform*. New York: Free Press, 1978.

Bimba, Anthony. *The History of the American Working-Class*. New York: International Publishers, 1927.

Bolling, Raynall. "The United States Steel Corporation and Labor." *Annals of the American Academy of Political and Social Science* 42 (July 1912).

Braverman, Harry. *Labor and Monopoly Capital*. New York: Modern Reader, 1974.

Brecher, Jeremy. *Strike!* San Francisco: Straightarrow Books, 1972.

Britt, D., and O. Galle. "Structural Antecedents of the Shape of Strikes: A Comparative Analysis." *American Sociological Review* 39 (October 1974).

Brody, David. *Labor in Crisis*. New York: J. P. Lippincott, 1965.

Brooks, Thomas. *Toil and Trouble*. New York: Delta Books, 1964.

Brubacher, John S., and Willis Rudy. *Higher Education in Transition*. 3rd Ed. New York: Harper and Row, 1976.

Burns, Arthur. *The Business Cycle in a Changing World*. New York: National Bureau of Economic Research, 1969.

Carey, Henry. *The Harmony of Interests*. Philadelphia: Henry Carey Baird and Co., 1890.

Carnegie, Andrew. "The Future of Labor." *Annals of the American Academy of Political and Social Science* 33 (March 1909).

Clark, V. S. *History of Manufactures in the United States*. 3 vols. New York: McGraw-Hill, 1929.

Cole, G.D.H. *A Short History of the English Working-Class*. London: Compton Printing Works, 1965.

Colletti, Lucio. *From Rousseau to Lenin: Studies in Ideology and Society*. New York: Monthly Review Press, 1972.

Collins, Randall. *Conflict Sociology*. New York: Basic Books, 1975.

Commager, Henry. *Lester Ward and the Welfare State*. New York: Bobbs-Merrill, 1967.

Commons, John. *A Documentary History of American Industrial Society*. 10 vols. Glendale, Calif.: Arthur H. Clark Co., 1910.

———. *Institutional Economics*. New York: Macmillan, 1934.

———. *Legal Foundations of Capitalism*. Madison: University of Wisconsin Press, 1968.

——. *Myself.* (1936). Madison: University of Wisconsin Press, 1963.

——. *Papers and Proceedings of the American Sociological Society.* December 1907.

——. *Races and Immigrants in America.* New York: Macmillan, 1907.

——, and John Andrews. *Principles of Labor Legislation.* (1916). 4th rev. ed. 1936. New York: Augustus M. Kelley, 1976.

Commons, John, and associates. *History of Labour in the United States.* 2 vols. New York: Macmillan, 1918.

Debs, Eugene. *Writings and Speeches of Eugene Debs.* New York: Hermitage Press, 1948.

Dick, William. *Labor and Socialism in America.* Port Washington, N.Y.: Kennikat Press, 1972.

Dorfman, Joseph, ed. *The Economic Mind in American Civilization.* New York: Viking Press, 1949.

——. *Two Essays by Henry Carter Adams.* New York: Augustus M. Kelley, 1969.

Dulles, Foster. *Labor in America.* New York: Thomas Crowell, 1966.

Dunlop, John. *Industrial Relations Systems.* New York: Henry Holt, 1958.

Durkheim, Emile. *The Division of Labor in Society.* New York: Free Press, 1933.

Edwards, Richards. *Contested Terrain.* New York: Basic Books, 1979.

Egbert, Donald, and Stow Persons, eds. *Socialism and American Life.* Vol. 1. Princeton: Princeton University Press, 1952.

Eliot, Charles. "Employers' Politics in the Industrial Strife." *Harper's* 110 (March 1905).

Ely, Richard. *Ground under Our Feet: An Autobiography.* New York: Macmillan, 1938.

——. *Introduction to Political Economy.* New York: Chautauqua Press, 1889.

——. *The Labor Movement.* New York: Thomas Crowell, 1886.

——. *Outlines of Economics.* New York: Chautauqua-Century Press, 1893.

——. *Socialism: An Examination of its Nature, its Strength and its Weaknesses with Suggestions for Social Reform.* New York: Thomas Crowell, 1894.

Evans, George. *Business Incorporations in the United States, 1800-1943.* New York: National Bureau of Economic Research, 1948.

Faulkner, Harold. *Economic History of the United States.* Vol. 7. New York: Holt, Rinehart and Winston, 1962.

Federal Writers' Project of the WPA, New Jersey—*A Guide to the Present and Past.* New York: Hastings House, 1946.

Fine, Sidney. *Laissez-Faire and the General Welfare State.* Ann Arbor: University of Michigan Press, 1956.

Fink, Gary. "The Rejection of Voluntarism." *Industrial and Labor Relations Review* 26, no. 2 (January 1973).

Fitch, John A. "The Explosion at Bayonne." *Survey* 37 (Oct. 21, 1916).

———. "When a Sheriff Breaks a Strike." *Survey* 34 (July 31, 1915).

Flugel, Felix, and Harold Faulkner. *Readings in the Economic and Social History of the United States*. New York: Harper & Bros. 1929.

Foner, Philip. *The Great Labor Uprising of 1877*. New York: Monad Press, 1977.

———. *History of the Labor Movement in the United States*. 4 vols. New York: International Publishers, 1965.

Frickey, Edwin. *Economic Fluctuations in the United States, 1866-1914*. New York: Russell & Russell, 1942.

Galenson, Walter, ed. *Comparative Labor Movements*. New York: Russell & Russell, 1968.

———. *Labor and Trade Unionism*. New York: John Wiley, 1960.

Garraty, John. "The United States Steel Corporation Versus Labor: The Early Years." *Labor History* 1 (Winter 1960).

Garrity, John, and J. Sternstein. *Encyclopedia of American Biography*. New York: Harper and Row, 1964.

Gibb, George, and Evelyn Knowlton. *The Resurgent Years, 1911-1927*. New York: Harper and Row, 1964.

Gompers, Samuel. *Seventy Years of Life and Labor*. 2 vols. New York: E. P. Dutton and Co., 1925.

Gordon, Arthur M. "Businessmen and Scholars." *Nation* 93 (Sept. 14, 1911).

Gouldner, Alvin. *The Future of Intellectuals and the Rise of the New Class*. New York: Seabury Press, 1979.

Graham, Hugh, and Ted Gurr. *Violence in America*. New York: Signet Books, 1969.

Gramsci, Antonio. *Prison Notebooks*. New York: International Publishers, 1972.

Green, Marguerite. *The National Civic Federation and the American Labor Movement, 1900-1925*. 1956. Reprint. Westport, Conn.: Greenwood Press, 1973.

Greenstone, J. D. *Labor in American Politics*. New York: Alfred Knopf, 1969.

Grob, Gerald. *Workers and Utopia*. Evanston, Ill.: Northwestern University Press, 1961.

Grossman, Henryk. "The Evolutionist Revolt Against Classical Economics." *The Journal of Political Economy* 51, no. 5 (October 1943) and 51, no. 6 (December 1943).

Gulick, Charles. *Labor Policy of the United States Steel Corporation*.

New York: Longmans, Green & Co., 1924.

Gurvitch, Georges, and W. Moore, eds. *Twentieth Century Sociology*. New York: The Philosophical Library, 1945.

Hacker, Louis. *The World of Andrew Carnegie*. New York: J. P. Lippincott, 1968.

Hamilton, Richard. *Class and Politics in the United States*. New York: John Wiley, 1972.

Haney, Lewis. *Business Organization and Combination*. New York: Macmillan, 1913.

Harter, Lafayette. "John R. Commons: Conservative or Liberal." *The Western Economic Journal* (Summer 1963).

Hegel, G.W.F. *The Phenomenology of Mind*. New York: Harper Torchbooks, 1967.

——. *The Philosophy of History*. New York: Dover Publications, 1956.

Henderson, C. R. "Business Men and Social Theorists." *American Journal of Sociology* 1 (January 1896).

Hillquit, Morris. *History of Socialism in the United States*. New York: Russell & Russell, 1965.

Hinkle, Roscoe, and Gisela Hinkle. *The Development of Modern Sociology*. New York: Random House, 1908.

Hobsbawm, E. J. *Labouring Men: Studies in the History of Labour*. New York: Basic Books, 1964.

Hobson, John. *The Evolution of Modern Capitalism*. New York: Macmillan, 1926.

Hofstadter, Richard. *Social Darwinism in American Thought*. Boston: Beacon Press, 1955.

Hopkins, C. Howard. *The Rise of the Social Gospel in American Protestantism*. New Haven: Yale University Press, 1967.

Horowitz, Irving. *The New Sociology*. New York: Oxford University Press, 1964.

Hoxie, Robert. *Trade Unionism in the United States*. New York: D. Appleton and Co., 1924.

Industrial Relations Research Association. *Interpreting the Labor Movement*. Madison, Wis., 1952.

Jerome, Harry. *Mechanization in Industry*. New York: National Bureau of Economic Research, 1934.

Jones, Otey S., in collaboration with Tim Ziobro. "A Short History of Bayonne, New Jersey." 1971. Unpublished manuscript in Municipal Library of Bayonne, N.J. New Jersey Reference Collection.

Karson, Marc. *American Labor Unions and Politics, 1900-1918*. Carbondale, Ill.: Southern Illinois University Press, 1958.

Kellogg, Paul. "Pioneering By Employers." *Survey* 26 (Aug. 19, 1911).

Kennedy, W. F. "John R. Commons, Conservative Reformer." *The Western Economic Journal* (Fall 1962).

Kerr, Clark; John Dunlop; Frederick Harbison; and Charles Meyers. *Industrialism and Industrial Man*. Cambridge: Harvard University Press, 1960.

Kirkland, Edward. *Dream and Thought in the Business Community*. Ithaca, N.Y.: Cornell University Press, 1956.

———. *Economic History of the United States*. Vol. 6. New York: Holt, Rinehart and Winston, 1947.

Korman, Gerd. *Industrialization, Immigrants and Americanizers*. Madison: State Historical Society of Wisconsin, 1967.

Kornhauser, Arthur; Robert Dubin; and Arthur Ross. *Industrial Conflict*. New York: McGraw-Hill, 1954.

Kuhn, Thomas. *The Structure of Scientific Revolutions*. Chicago: University of Chicago Press, 1971.

Lane, F. Van Z. *Bayonne, New Jersey: Its Location, Industries, Advantages, and History*. Bayonne, N.J.: Chamber of Commerce, 1916.

Laslett, John. *Labor and the Left*. New York: Basic Books, 1970.

Lester, Richard. *As Unions Mature*. Princeton: Princeton University Press, 1958.

Levitt, Theodore. "Prosperity Versus Strikes." *Industrial and Labor Relations Review* 6, no. 2 (January 1953).

Lichtheim, George, *The Concept of Ideology and other Essays*. New York: Random House, 1967.

Lindblom, Charles. *Unions and Capitalism*. New Haven: Yale University Press, 1949.

Lipset, S. M. *The First New Nation*. New York: Basic Books, 1963.

Livesay, Harold. *Samuel Gompers and Organized Labor in America*. Boston: Little, Brown and Co., 1978.

Lukacs, Georg. *History and Class Consciousness*. London: Merlin Press, 1971.

McLaughlin, Barry, ed. *Studies in Social Movements*. New York: Free Press, 1969.

McNulty, Paul. *The Origins and Development of Labor Economics*. Cambridge: MIT Press, 1980.

Madison, Charles. *American Labor Leaders*. New York: Frederick Unger, 1962.

Mannheim, Karl. *Ideology and Utopia*. New York: Harcourt Brace Jovanovich, 1964.

Marx, Karl. *Capital*. 3 vols. New York: International Publishers, 1963.

———. *Grundrisse*. New York: Vintage Books, 1973.

Marx, Karl, and Friedrich Engels. *The German Ideology*. New York: International Publishers, 1972.

———. *The Holy Family*. Moscow: Progress Publishers, 1975.

Meek, R. L. *Studies in the Labour Theory of Value*. London: Laurence and Wishart, 1958.

Mergen, Bernard. "Blacksmiths and Welders: Identity and Phenomenal Chance." *Industrial and Labor Relations Review* 25, no. 3 (April 1972).

Mills, C. W. *The Power Elite*. New York: Oxford University Press, 1956.

———. *The Sociological Imagination*. New York: Oxford University Press, 1959.

———. *Sociology and Pragmatism*. New York: Oxford University Press, 1966.

———. *White Collar*. New York: Oxford University Press, 1956.

Mitchell, Wesley. *Business Cycles*. New York: National Bureau of Economic Research, 1927.

Montgomery, David. "The 'New Unionism' and the Transformation of Workers' Consciousness in America, 1909-1922." *Journal of Social History* (Summer 1974).

———. *Workers' Control in America*. New York: Cambridge University Press, 1979.

Moore, Barrington. *Social Origins of Dictatorship and Democracy*. Boston: Beacon Press, 1966.

Moore, Wilbert. *Industrialization and Labor—Social Aspects of Economic Development*. Ithaca, N.Y.: Cornell University Press, 1957.

———. *Industrialization and the Social Order*. New York: Macmillan, 1955.

Morris, James. *Conflict within the AFL: A Study of Craft Versus Industrial Unionism, 1901-1938*. Ithaca, N.Y.: Cornell University Press, 1958.

Mulkay, Michael. *Science and the Sociology of Knowledge*. London: George Allen & Unwin, 1979.

Murray, Robert. *Red Scare: A Study in National Hysteria, 1919-1920*. 1955. Reprint. Westport, Conn.: Greenwood Press, 1980.

Nevins, Allan. *Study in Power: John D. Rockefeller, Industrialist and Philanthropist*. 2 vols. New York: Charles Scribner, 1953.

Newman, Philip. *The Development of Economic Thought*. Englewood Cliffs: Prentice-Hall, 1952.

Noble, David. "Review of Lafayette Harter's *John R. Commons: His Assault on Laissez-Faire*." *Labor History* 4 (Fall 1963).

North, Douglas. *The Economic Growth of the United States, 1790-1860*. Englewood Cliffs: Prentice-Hall, 1961.

Ossowski, Stanley. *Class Structure in the Social Consciousness*. New York: Free Press, 1963.

Page, Charles. *Class and American Sociology*. New York: Shocken Books, 1969.

Parker, Carleton. "The Labor Policy of the American Trusts (1914)."
   Atlantic Monthly 125 (February 1920).

Pelling, Henry. *A Short History of the Labour Party.* New York: St.
   Martin's Press, 1965.

Perlman, Mark. *Labor Unions Theories in America.* Evanston, Ill.: Free
   Press, 1958.

Perlman, Selig. *A History of Trade Unionism in the United States.* New
   York: Augustus M. Kelley, 1950.

——. *A Theory of the Labor Movement.* New York: Augustus M. Kelley,
   1949.

Perlman, Selig, and Philip Taft. *History of Labor in the United States,
   1896-1932.* New York: Macmillan, 1935.

Peterson, Florence. "Strikes in the United States, 1880-1936." Bulletin
   651. Washington, D.C.: Department of Labor, Bureau of Labor
   Statistics, 1937.

Prezioso, Donald. "The Oil Industry in Bayonne: Its Rise & Decline."
   1976. Unpublished manuscript in Municipal Library of Bayonne,
   N.J. New Jersey Reference Collection.

Pritchett, Henry S. "The Policy of the Carnegie Foundation for the Advancement of Teaching." *Educational Review* 32 (June 1906).

——. "Shall the University Become a Business Corporation?" *Atlantic
   Monthly* 96 (September 1905).

Rader, Benjamin. *The Academic Mind and Reform.* Lexington: University
   of Kentucky Press, 1966.

Reynolds, Larry, and Reynolds, Janice. *The Sociology of Sociology.*
   New York: McKay, 1970.

Rockefeller, John D., Jr. "Labor and Capital—Partners." *Atlantic Monthly*
   117 (January 1916).

Ross, Arthur, and Paul Hartman. *Changing Patterns of Industrial Conflict.*
   New York: John Wiley, 1960.

Rowan, Richard, and Herbert Northrup. *Readings in Labor Economics
   and Labor Relations.* Homewood, Ill.: Richard Irwin, 1968.

Rudolph, Frederick. *The American College and University: A History.*
   New York: Knopf, 1962.

Saposs, David. *Communism in American Unions.* New York: McGraw-
   Hill, 1959.

Schucking, Levin. *The Sociology of Literary Taste.* 1923. Reprint.
   Chicago: University of Chicago Press, 1966.

Schumpeter, Joseph. *Capitalism, Socialism, and Democracy.* New York:
   Harper Brothers, 1950.

——. *Business Cycles. A Theoretical, Historical, & Statistical Analysis of
   the Capitalist Process.* New York: McGraw-Hill, 1939.

———. *History of Economic Analysis*. New York: Oxford University Press, 1961.

Schwab, Charles. "Capital and Labor." *Annals of the American Academy of Political & Social Science* 81 (January 1919).

Schwendinger, Herman, and Julia Schwendinger. *The Sociologists of the Chair*. New York: Basic Books, 1974.

Seckler, David. "The Naivete of John R. Commons." *The Western Economic Journal* (Summer 1966).

———. *Thorstein Veblen and the Institutionalists*. Boulder: Colorado Associated University Press, 1975.

Skeels, Jack. "Measures of U.S. Strike Activity." *Industrial and Labor Relations Review* 24, no. 4 (July 1971).

Snyder, David. "Institutional Setting and Industrial Conflict: Comparative Analyses of France, Italy and the United States." *American Sociological Review* 40 (June 1975).

Soule, George. *The Economic History of the United States*. Vol. 8. New York: Holt, Rinehart and Winston, 1947.

Spence, Clark. *The Sinews of American Capitalism*. New York: Hill and Wang, 1974.

Stern, R. N. "Intermetropolitan Patterns of Strike Frequency." *Industrial and Labor Relations Review* 29 (January 1966).

Sweezy, Paul. *The Theory of Capitalist Development*. New York: Monthly Review Press, 1964.

Taft, Philip. *The A.F. of L. in the Time of Gompers*. New York: Harper & Bros., 1957.

———. "Attempts to Radicalize the Labor Movement." *Industrial and Labor Relations Review* 1, no. 4 (July 1948).

———. *Organized Labor in American History*. New York: Harper and Row, 1969.

Tannenbaum, Frank. *A Philosophy of Labor*. New York: Alfred Knopf, 1951.

Thompson, E. P. *The Making of the English Working-Class*. New York: Vintage Books, 1963.

———. *The Poverty of Theory and other Essays*. New York: Monthly Review Press, 1975.

Touraine, Alain. *Workers' Attitudes to Technical Change*. Organization For Economic Co-operation and Development, 1965.

Turner, Ralph, and Lewis Killian. *Collective Behavior*. Englewood Cliffs: Prentice-Hall, 1972.

Ulman, Lloyd. *The Rise of the National Trade Union*. Cambridge: Harvard University Press, 1955.

Veysey, Laurence. *The Emergence of the American University*. Chicago:

University of Chicago Press, 1965.

Ware, Norman. *The Industrial Worker, 1840-1860*. Chicago: Quadrangle Books, 1964.

————. *Labor Movement in the United States, 1860-1895*. New York: D. Appleton Co., 1929.

Webster American Biographies. Springfield, Mass.: G. and C. Merriam Co., 1974.

Wiebe, Robert. *Businessmen and Reform*. Cambridge: Harvard University Press, 1962.

————. *The Search for Order*. New York: Hill and Wang, 1967.

Wilensky, Harold. *Intellectuals in Labor Unions*. Glencoe, Ill.: Free Press, 1956.

Williams, William Appleton. *The Contours of American History*. New York: World, 1961.

Williamson, Harold, ed. *The Growth of the American Economy*. New York: Prentice-Hall, 1951.

Wolman, Leo. *Ebb and Flow in Trade Unionism*. New York: National Bureau of Economic Research, 1936.

————. *The Growth of American Trade Unionism, 1880-1923*.

Wright, Philip G. "Contest in Congress Between Organized Labor and Business." *Quarterly Journal of Economics* 29 (February 1915).

Yellowitz, Irwin. *The Position of the Worker in American Society, 1865-96*. Englewood Cliffs: Prentice-Hall, 1969.

Yoder, Dale. "Economic Changes & Industrial Unrest in the United States." *Journal of Political Economy* 48 (1940).

Zeitlin, Irving. *Ideology and the Development of Sociological Theory*. Englewood Cliffs: Prentice-Hall, 1968.

Unsigned Articles

"Bloodshed in Labor Wars." *Literary Digest* 57 (Aug. 7, 1915).

"The Burning Issue of Free Speech at Eastern As Well As Western Universities." *Current Opinion* 59 (August 1915).

"Collective Bargaining and Colorado." *Survey* 33 (Jan. 16, 1915).

"Conflicting Labor Policy." *New Republic* 14 (Feb. 16, 1918).

"The End of the Bayonne Strike." *The Independent* 88 (Oct. 30, 1916).

"Freedom of Speech and Political Issues at Western State Universities." *Current Opinion* 58 (June 1915).

"Newspaper Incitement to Violence." *New Republic* 8 (Oct. 21, 1916).

"Pro-Labor Pleas From Capitalists." *Literary Digest* 50 (Feb. 6, 1915).

"Report of the Committee of the American Association of University Professors on Academic Freedom and Academic Tenure." *School Society* 3 (Jan. 22, 1916).

Newspapers

The Evening Review. Bayonne, N.J. (Oct. 7-20, 1916).
The Jersey Journal. Jersey City, N.J. (July 20-28, 1915).
The New York Call. New York, N.Y. (July 19-30, 1915.)

About the Author

John A. DeBrizzi has written articles on social theory and labor which have appeared in *Telos*, *Berkeley Journal of Sociology*, *Journal of the History of Sociology*, and *Studies in Soviet Thought*.